THE NEW HUMANITY

THE NEW HUMANITY

BRUCE KENRICK

COLLINS
ST JAMES'S PLACE, LONDON
1958

For Isabel

PREFACE

I AM indebted to Doctor John A. Mackay whose kind invitation to engage in post-graduate study at Princeton Theological Seminary provided me with the opportunity of doing much of the work on which this book is based. I am also obliged to the Faculty of the Seminary for permission to publish, in a somewhat different form, some chapters of a thesis which I wrote during my stay in Princeton.

To the Westminster Foundation of the University of California, Berkeley, I acknowledge a special debt of gratitude for the generous hospitality afforded me during the summer of 1955 when the first part of this book was revised. I am also indebted to the University for use of the Libraries during that period.

I wish to express my warmest thanks to the Rev. Professor James S. Stewart who read the book in manuscript, offered valuable suggestions, and was generous enough to write the Foreword. The manuscript was also read by the Rev. G. J. Ainger, of Loughton, Essex; Professor Paul L. Lehmann of Harvard University; the Rev. Professor William Stewart of Serampore College; and Miss L. M. Burtt, formerly of Yenching University and now of Bangalore: I thank them all sincerely. I am also indebted to Miss E. A. Robertson who gave expert help with the proofs.

Much that is written in these pages owes its inspiration to a number of communities in whose work and thought I have been privileged to share. I must especially mention the Mission de France, the East Harlem Protestant Parish, the Little Brothers of Jesus, and the Christavashram, Travancore.

PREFACE

I am deeply grateful to the Members for their hospitality, their friendship, and their counsel. When time permits, I hope to give some account of the ways in which the theological position outlined in this study is finding flesh and blood expression in such courageous ventures as these.

BRUCE KENRICK

Chinsura,
West Bengal
1957

FOREWORD

THE AUTHOR of this work, who is a graduate of Edinburgh and Princeton and now a servant of the Church in India, has put us in his debt by setting forth so clearly in these pages what may be called a "theology of identification." It is no disembodied Gospel that is presented here, but one that bears at every point upon the pattern and structure of daily life and common experience. This is immensely important; for when we hear charges of irrelevance and unreality brought against Christianity to-day, we cannot but realise that part at least of the blame must lie at the door of a false spirituality which has tended to separate faith from life and to dissociate religion from material and mundane concerns. I find particularly helpful the writer's insistence that the vocation of the Christian involves a threefold identification—with Christ, with the Church, with the world. The argument is presented throughout with such a verve and vigour, such a degree of personal concern and urgency, that it is bound to make a deep impression on the reader's mind. Here is a book with a most cogent and compelling message for to-day.

JAMES S. STEWART

New College,
The University of Edinburgh

CONTENTS

INTRODUCTION   *page* 13

PART ONE

THE NATURE OF THE CHURCH

I   THE WORD BECAME FLESH   19

II THE BODY OF CHRIST   31

III THE HEAD OF THE BODY   43

IV A SPIRITUAL BODY   66

PART TWO

"THEREFORE . . ."

V   SO SEND I YOU   84

VI   THAT THEY MAY HAVE LIFE   103

VII YE SHALL BE FREE INDEED   128

VIII A NEW CREATION   149

     CONCLUSION   179

     INDEX OF NAMES   183

     INDEX OF SUBJECTS   184

     INDEX OF BIBLICAL REFERENCES   187

INTRODUCTION

ON THE frontiers of the Church's life, in the East as in the West, one meets men who are possessed with a boundless hope and a disturbing confidence. Their lives bear witness to their profound conviction that the Church stands on the threshold of a new Springtime in which she can become, in every realm of life, that revolutionary force which Christ means her to be.

Most men admire their conviction and their life. But few can translate admiration into action. For, unlike those who are living on the frontier, most of us are thinking in terms of evangelistic strategy, or of social action, or of sanctification. The frontiersmen are thinking in terms of Jesus Christ and His Church. In thought and action they are finding an answer to the fundamental question—What is the Church? They are convinced that the Church's deepest need is to understand herself in terms of her essential nature, and to work out the implications of that nature in her life in the world. The first task, they affirm, is not to know what evangelism, social action, and sanctification are ; these become substantial, powerful and relevant only when they are the supernatural expressions of the life of a Church which knows what she is in her innermost being.

There is a widespread fear amongst Christians that to think of the Church in terms of her essential being is to adopt a dangerous mode of thought which rests upon a static and non-temporal conception of the Church. The tendency is, therefore, to avoid thinking at all in terms of the Church's essence. But this tendency is itself fraught with much graver dangers than those it seeks to avoid. Whenever the Church is selective in her approach to truth, whenever she chooses to investigate and expose herself only to those aspects of truth which, she affirms, will not endanger her own life—then the Church stands in peril of losing the very life she seeks to preserve and in danger of dictating to God the limits of her own being.

The Church must seek the *truth*. She must not seek only that which she decides will be convenient and useful for her continuing life. She must not impose limits upon her search for truth. She must seek the truth in all its fulness, and especially that truth which pertains to her own deepest nature.

The tragic weakness of the Church in great areas of her life to-day has its roots in this perplexing predicament— the Church knows perfectly well how she is supposed to *act*, but because the Church does not know what she *is*, she is unable to act. The Church knows what God demands of her. But because she does not know what God has made her, she lacks the power to obey. The Church lives by faith. And biblical faith is never primarily faith in a divine imperative. It is first and foremost faith in a divine indicative. God commanded Moses to lead the children of Israel out of bondage into the promised land. But this divine imperative had its roots in the divine indicative— " Certainly I will be with thee."[1] When the risen Christ commanded His disciples to preach the Gospel unto every nation, the divine imperative rested squarely upon the divine indicative—" Lo, I am with you always, even unto the end of the world." But more than this : with God's

[1] Ex. 3 : 12.

14

personal intervention in history an accomplished fact, the divine imperative was given infinitely deeper roots. Both the imperative and the indicative went deep down into an ontological reality which had been accomplished in the Incarnation, the Cross and the Resurrection. Christ had made His Church *one* with Himself. There had been at-*one*-ment. The ' Go ye ' and the ' Lo, I am with you ' found their ultimate and substantial dynamic in a relation of *being* between the risen Christ and His Church.

Hence, the greatest need of the Christian is not to know what he is supposed to *do*. His greatest need is to know who he *is*. Like the Church, he lives by faith. And there can be no faith without knowledge. Well did Isaiah cry— " My people are gone into captivity, because they have no knowledge." [1] Small wonder that a Church, knowing so little of what she is in her innermost nature, so often presents a pale, weak, anæmic aspect, ' having a form of godliness, but denying the power thereof.' [2]

It is largely because of this fundamental ignorance that, for multitudes outside and inside the fold, the Church seems quite irrelevant to-day. ' Some like art and they go to the studio. Some like drama and they go to the theatre. Some like religion and they go to Church.' [3] Too often the Church is no more than a place where like-minded men and women meet for an hour each week. It is a religious club. The conduct of the baptised seems to be much the same as that of the unbaptised. The offence, the scandal, the shock and the power which gripped and held the pagan Roman Empire has far too often vanished away and the ghost of the Church remains.

We may be sure that the ghost will not gain flesh and blood until it is thought of, not primarily in terms of its

---

[1] Isa. 5 : 13.   [2] 2 Tim. 3 : 5.   [3] cf. George Macleod, *Only One Way Left*, Iona Community, 1956, p. 3.

obligations, but in terms of Jesus Christ who is both its essence and its Lord. The Church which lives in constant dependence upon her Saviour Jesus Christ must know herself to be a Church whose nature is identical with His nature. She partakes in His divine humanity. Her being is His being. This relation in being with the eternal Son of God is not one which is dependent, in the first place, on faith—'Man's search for God.' The movement is the other way around. It is dependent upon the *divine* initiative. It is dependent upon God's having become once for all and irreversibly partaker in our sinful human nature.[1] So that His life is our life, His attributes are our attributes, His mission is our mission.

This is the ultimate truth about the Church. This, with its staggering implications, is what we mean when we confess, 'The Word became flesh.'

[1] Ro. 8 : 3.

Part One

THE NATURE OF
THE CHURCH

CHAPTER ONE

THE WORD BECAME FLESH

THE WHOLE of the Gospel is contained in the phrase—
'The Word became flesh.' Man's salvation was accomplished in this never-to-be-repeated event in which God Himself, in the Person of the Son, took human, fallen, sinful[1] flesh. By the Incarnation, the flesh and blood of man became what it had never been before. It became nothing less than the flesh and blood of God.

If this were all, it were enough. 'If the contemporary generation (of Jesus) had left nothing behind them but these words : "We have believed that in such and such a year God appeared among us in the humble figure of a servant, that he lived and taught in our community, and finally died," it would be more than enough.'[2] Properly understood, these words of Kierkegaard enshrine the central truth of the Gospel. They affirm that, when God acts, He acts in a decisive, irreversible way. He acted in the Incarnation. And He acted in such a way that humanity was bound to divinity in absolute, flesh and blood reality so that man can never be the same again. *God* became *man* !

The eternal Son of God did not merely take upon Himself the *form*, the outward form, of a man.[3] He became

---

[1] Ro. 8 : 3.   [2] S. Kierkegaard, *Philosophical Fragments*, Princeton University Press, 1952 p. 87.   [3] cf. A. M. Ramsey, *The Glory of God and the Transfiguration of Christ*, p. 54, μορφή means *real being* in contrast with outward appearance.   Thus

real man with all his limitations. God was not play acting when He sent His Son. He was not mocking man with a sham 'becoming.' He was in earnest when He sought our salvation. Christ became fully man.

Unless this be so, there is no salvation. If there are any reservations in the humanity of Jesus Christ, God has *not* become man. Not the man whom *we* call 'man.' If He were immune from the least or the greatest of my temptations, not only do *I* cry with Peter, " I know not the man ! " But *Christ* must say of *me*, " I know not this man ! " He must say, " I have not entered into his estate nor can I comprehend it. I cannot bear his sin nor can I carry his humanity into heaven." If Christ's flesh were not as human as my flesh, then it were some strange, alien, fearful flesh which has no communion with this fallen flesh of mine.

But it was a *real* becoming. We observe, in the first place, that the flesh which God took at the incarnation was mortal, sinful flesh. Otherwise Christ could not have died. 'God sending his own Son in the likeness of sinful flesh,' [1] that is to say ἐν ὁμοιώματι σαρκὸς ἁμαρτίας, flesh that *belonged* to sin. The nature which He took was uncompromisingly human. It was our sinful nature. Only so could He save. ' The nature which God took in Christ is identical with our nature under the Fall,' writes Karl Barth.[2] ' Christ,' he continues, ' was no sinner. But his situation was, both from within and without, that of a sinner. He freely entered upon solidarity with our lost and wretched state. So and only so could the revelation of God to us, our reconciliation with him, take place in him and

---

Romans 12 : 2. ' Be not outwardly fashioned (συνσχηματίζεσθε) according to this world ; but be ye changed *in real being* (μεταμορφοῦσθε) by the renewing of your mind.' Quoted by J. A. T. Robinson, *The Body*, S.C.M., 1952, p. 39. *Op. cit.*

[1] Ro. 8 : 3.   [2] *Dogmatik* 1, 2, 168. Quoted by J. A. T. Robinson.

through him.'[1] Otherwise the temptations of our Lord would be nothing more than a hollow sham. Whereas, in fact, he 'was in all points tempted like as we are.'[2] Paul insists that the human nature of Jesus Christ was precisely the same as our own; and at the same time he makes it very plain that He was entirely sinless. His flesh was sinful flesh. He even goes so far as to affirm that God 'made Him to be *sin* for us'[3] but he immediately follows this statement with the most positive assertion that He 'knew no sin.'[3]

The reality of this 'becoming' man is seen with even greater clarity when we turn to the Gospel narratives. The picture there presented is of the divine Son of God who was, at the same time, as human as His disciples were human. We see a life of constant temptation ('the devil ... departed from Him *for a season*').[4] We see Him weeping by the grave of His friend. We see Him hungry, weary, footsore, sad. We see Him torn with doubts as the Cross looms large before Him—'Father, save me from this hour.'[5] We see Him engaged in a conflict of wills; His own will over against His Father's—'O my Father, let this cup pass from me! Nevertheless, not my will, but thine be done.'[6] We see Him bruised and bleeding, mocked and scourged, stumbling up the via dolorosa to meet an ignominious end. We hear a very human cry of dereliction—'My God, my God, why hast thou forsaken me?'[7] We see a limp and lifeless figure—dead, upon a tree. Behold the man!

The ruthless honesty of the Gospel writers leaves us in no doubt that the Christ whom *they* knew was bone of our bone and flesh of our flesh. He was, in His human nature, no less and no more than fully man. And we do Him no honour to affirm that His humanity was 'better' than our

---

[1] Op. cit. p. 166. [2] Heb. 4: 15. [3] 2 Co. 5: 21. [4] Lu. 4: 13. [5] Jn. 12: 27.
[6] Mt. 26: 39.   Lu. 22; 42; cf. Jn. 5: 30; 6: [38. [7] Mk. 15: 34.

humanity. The wonder of His sinless life was that He carried sinful flesh unblemished to the end.

Throughout His life we see our Lord entering more and more deeply into the life of sinful man. He exposes Himself unreservedly to man. He gives Himself to man. He intertwines His holy life with the life of sinful man. He interpenetrates the whole of man's existence in such a final and irreversible way that He is bound to man for ever.

This gracious movement of the incarnation was foreshadowed in the Old Testament priesthood. When Aaron entered the holiest of holies, he did not only bear upon his forehead a plate of pure gold with the inscription, ' Holiness to the Lord.' He also bore upon his heart the Urim and the Thummim. On these two stones were engraved the names of the twelve tribes of Israel. Aaron carried them all in his breast. He identified himself with them. He agonised in prayer for them before the Lord. *He* ' bore the judgment of the children of Israel upon his heart before the Lord continually.' [1] He stood before God on their behalf, bowed down with the weight of their sins.[2] Thus identified with all Israel, he was their Representative Man. The glory of his priesthood (which shone from his forehead as he came forth from the sanctuary) pointed forward to the glory of the Great High Priest who was to come forth from the heaven of heavens and who was so to identify Himself with all men as to carry them on His heart and in His body through death and hell and into the Kingdom which God had promised to Abraham, to Isaac and to Jacob.

The whole life of Christ presses forward to a complete and unbreakable solidarity with men which reaches its climax on the Cross. Right at the outset of His ministry

[1] Ex. 28 : 30.   [2] Ex. 28 : 12.

He submits Himself to the baptism of John. This was a baptism for one kind of person only. It was for sinners. "I have need to be baptised of *thee*," cried John, "and comest thou to *me*?" But the Christ of God would not by-pass man's deepest humiliation. He received the baptism for sinners.

From the baptism of water to the baptism in blood we see an ever deepening identification of Christ with man. The core of man's problem was the conflict between good and evil. This conflict Christ took into His very heart. His sinful flesh knew the longing to be faithful and the hourly temptation to be faithless. He penetrated into the depths of man's situation. He became bound up with men in their sin, touched with their infirmities, bowed down with their griefs. He interpenetrated the whole of man's life and was thus made perfect. That is to say that He achieved perfect solidarity with sinners. His life became inextricably bound up with theirs. He and they became *one*. There was at-one-ment.

Not only do we see this 'identification' in the daily life and actions of our Lord. We see it very clearly in His words. And nowhere does it stand out with greater clarity than in the title which He chose for Himself and used consistently throughout His ministry—Son of Man. At every turning point in His life, when men wondered who He was, why He had come and what He was doing, He proclaimed the truth about Himself by using this title. At Cæsarea Philippi; 'Whom say ye that I, the Son of Man, am?' As He descended from the Mount of Transfiguration; 'Tell the vision to no man, until the Son of Man be risen again from the dead.' As He constituted the Church in the Upper Room; 'The Son of Man goeth as it is written of Him; but woe unto that man by whom the Son of Man is betrayed.' And on the last day when he stood, accused, before the high priest; ' " Art thou the Christ, the Son of the Blessed ? " And Jesus said, " I am : and ye shall see the Son of Man sitting on the right hand of power, and coming in the clouds of heaven." '

What lies behind our Lord's use of this title ? Does it throw any light on the nature of His ' becoming ' flesh, on His identification of Himself with sinful man ?

The title is found in the Similitudes of Enoch, in 1 Esdras, in Ezekiel and in Daniel. In the Similitudes of Enoch, the Son of Man has the attributes of a pre-existent, heavenly Messiah, the ancient Davidic prince and the prophetic servant of the Lord. The Son of Man of 1 Esdras is one who comes to found a universal, supra-national Kingdom. But it is when we come to examine Ezekiel's use of the title that we begin to enter into the inner-most meaning of it and see how it affirmed the solidarity of Christ with sinful man.

The Son of Man in Ezekiel is a chosen vessel of the Lord, he is one who is sent with a message for all mankind ; but, at the same time, he is a humble human figure who takes his place in the midst of the squalor of this world, one who has no rights of his own, one who is unreservedly ' man,' whose flesh is our flesh, whose sorrows are our sorrows, who enters fully into the bondage and captivity of men.[1] The title thus implies a radical identification of Christ with all mankind.

There can be no doubt, however, that the title was associated, in the mind of our Lord, with the Danielic figure more than with any other. And here we enter into the very heart of the matter.

The Son of Man in Daniel is not one who enjoys

[1] Ez. 3 : 15.

24

solidarity with the whole human race. He is identified with the chosen people of God. That this Danielic figure was central in the mind of Jesus can be seen from the fact that, in moments of high crisis, He spoke of Himself as Son of Man in words which were virtually identical with those of the prophet.[1] Thus He addresses the chosen few at Cæsarea Philippi; thus, when His disciples came to Him privately,[2] He spoke with deep emotion of the last judgment; and thus He addressed the high priest of the people of Israel when He stood, forsaken and alone, at the judgment seat of man.

The supreme significance of the Danielic figure is to be found in the fact that it refers *both* to the Son of Man and *also* to the saints of the Most High.[3] The Son of Man is identical with the saints. The figure which is to receive the kingdom is a single personality. It is also the saints of God. The Son of Man receives ' an everlasting dominion, which shall not pass away.' (v. 14). This dominion which is *eternally* His also belongs *eternally* to the saints—' the dominion . . . shall be given to the people of the saints of the Most High; their kingdom shall be an everlasting kingdom, and all dominions shall serve and obey them.' (v. 27 A.R.S.V.). It is clear that when the prophet is speaking about the Son of Man he is also speaking about the saints. The two are inextricably bound up together. The Son of Man and his saints are *one*.

It is not surprising that Christ chose this title. He, the Son of Man, was so to live and so to die as to unite Himself for ever with the chosen people. He was so to identify Himself with them that, when speaking of Him one would be speaking of them and when speaking of them one would be speaking of Him. This was the Man into whom the

---

[1] Dan. 7: 13; cf. Mk. 14: 62; Mt. 25: 31; 16: 27, etc.   [2] Mat. 24: 30.
[3] Dan. 7: 13, 14, 18.

Remnant was to be ingrafted in such a way that it would be spoken of as His Body.

But this identity of saints and Saviour awaited its completion. It was not made perfect when the Word became flesh, nor in the life which the Apostle's Creed describes by the single word, ' suffered,' nor was it perfected by a verbal identification of Christ with His people. It awaited consummation in real, historical *action*—in baptism, in the eucharist and on the Cross.

Baptism. Jesus had set His face to go up to Jerusalem, and on the road He told the twelve that He was about to meet His death which, He affirmed, would be the prelude to His resurrection.[1] It is at this point that the discourse with James and John commences. They ask that they may be allowed to share in Christ's glory. " Can ye drink of the cup that I drink of," asks Jesus, " and be baptised with the baptism that I am baptised with ? " And to our surprise the disciples reply, " We can ! " But we are even more surprised when our Lord declares, " Ye shall indeed drink of the cup that I drink of ; and with the baptism that I am baptised withal shall ye be baptised ! "[2] This was to affirm unequivocally that the disciples were in fact to share in the death and the glory of their Lord. The baptism with which He had been baptised in water had been a baptism not only unto glory but unto suffering ; for the same Voice which hailed Him as Son of God also proclaimed Him to be the Suffering Servant of Isaiah 42 and 53.[3] The baptism which awaited Him in Jerusalem was a baptism of blood, ' and how am I straitened until it be accomplished ! '[4] It was a baptism which led to the Cross. *This* was the baptism with which He was to be baptised. And *this*, our Lord affirmed, was the baptism in which His

[1] Mk. 10 :34. [2] Mk. 10 : 38 ff. [3] Mk. 1 : 11. Psa. 2 : 7. Isa. 42 : 1, 53 : 10.
[4] Lu. 12 : 50.

26

disciples were to share! They were to be one body with Him in His baptism of death. This is, indeed, a ' hard saying.' What is Christ's meaning here? It is as though He anticipates our astonishment and adds another sign to that already given.

" Can ye drink of the cup that I drink of? Yes, indeed —ye shall! " He declares. What is this ' cup '? A hint is given in Isaiah 51 where we hear of the ' cup of his fury, dregs of the cup of trembling.' [1] But the nature of this cup is made explicit when we hear Jesus in prayer in the Garden of Gethsemane, faced with the fearful prospect of the Cross and confronted with the horror of bearing in His body the full weight of His Father's judgment. There, with His soul sore troubled, He cries out to heaven, " Father, if it be possible, let this *cup* pass from me! " [2] There can be no reasonable doubt that the cup to which He refers is the cup of suffering which He must drain upon the Cross. And, He declares, *this* is the cup which His disciples shall drink. *They* will be baptised upon the Cross! *They* will drink the cup of suffering on the tree! How can these things be?

The Eucharist. Our thought moves to the Upper Room. And again we hear the voice of Jesus, " Take, eat, this is my body." [3] And, after the bread, He passes the cup (the *cup*!) saying, " This is my blood of the new covenant, which is shed for many.[4] Drink ye all of it." [5] They ate His broken body. They drank His blood. *He* entered *them*. They did not enter Him. He entered them. His flesh became their flesh. His blood became their blood. He incorporated them into His body. They *became* His body! The body of which He is the Head.

Indeed, they rose from that table as the Body of Christ —redeemed by Him who was their Head. Redeemed for

---

[1] Isa. 51 : 17; cf. Zech. 12 : 2. [2] Mt. 26 : 39. [3] Mk. 14 : 22. [4] Mk. 14 : 24, A.R.S.V. [5] Mt. 26 : 27.

all eternity. It is true that no more than a few brief hours had passed before they had all forsaken Him and fled. Yet they were still redeemed. They were still His Body. For they had not chosen Him. *He* had chosen them. And, in the Eucharist, He had not only constituted His Church, He had identified Himself with His Church in such an unconditional way that, for ever after, come what may, everything that happened to Him would also happen to them. Christ and His Church were one.

The Cross. 'Ye shall indeed drink of the cup that I drink of; and with the baptism that I am baptised withal shall ye be baptised.' They were to limp to Calvary. The disciples were to die upon the tree. And yet, when we turn our gaze upon the Cross, we do not see the broken body of John and we do not see the outpoured blood of James. *We* do not see them. But *God* does !

Our minds are almost overwhelmed by the depths of this mystery. Yet from it all one great truth shines forth. When Christ was crucified on a hill outside a city wall— *we* were there. We were not merely standing at the foot of the Cross, not merely driving the nails into His hands and feet, not merely mocking Him, spitting in His face— we were there in His body on the tree. When the judgment of God fell on His Son—we were there in His body on the tree.

Not that we thus *earned* our salvation. Not that *we* achieved anything on the Cross. We achieved as little as the faithless disciples who abandoned their Lord and fled. Yet as surely as He had made them one with Him, as surely as He had incorporated them for ever into His body at the sacred feast, as surely as they, the members of His body, were baptised with Him upon the Cross and drank with Him the cup of suffering on the tree—just as surely are we persuaded that *we* died there with Him.

But not only did we *die* there with Him. As we have already seen, the baptism of our Lord was unto suffering and also unto glory. So that as we share His baptism and as we partake of His body and His blood we are also made partakers of His glory. Not only do James and John reign now in heaven with Him. The whole Church reigns with Him.

There are but two places in the New Testament where we hear the words ' Son of Man ' when they are not on the lips of Jesus. One is in the vision given to John in exile on the island of Patmos [1] and the other is in the vision given to Stephen as he died a martyr's death.[2] In both cases this Son of Man, who had gathered into His own body the saints of the Most High—in both cases He is the one who is regnant over history.[3] He is the One with whom we sit in heavenly places at the right hand of God even now.[4] And when He returns upon the clouds of glory to perfect the ingrafting of His faithful people into His New Humanity, we shall *already* be in Him.

From the moment when God invaded history and took our flesh at Bethlehem, right through His life of unqualified self-giving and on to the Last Supper and the final moment on the Cross, Jesus Christ was entering into full and final solidarity with the whole of human nature so that our flesh is bound unreservedly to His flesh and His flesh is bound unreservedly to our flesh. He fashioned a New Humanity in His own human body. And He fashioned it in such a way that His New Humanity is *our* New Humanity—His body is our body. This is the body which rose in glory from the dead. This is the body

---

[1] Rev. 1 : 13.   [2] Acts 7 : 56.   [3] Wm. Manson ' *Epistle to the Hebrews,*' p. 32.   [4] Eph. 2 : 6.

which ascended into heaven and which was presented faultless before the presence of God's glory with exceeding joy. This is the body which ' will so come in like manner as ye have seen Him go into heaven.[1] This is the Body of Christ. And the Body of Christ is the Church.

[1] Acts 1 : 11 ; cf. Jn. 17 : 23 ff ; 15 : 4 ff.

CHAPTER TWO

THE BODY OF CHRIST

WHEN PAUL described the Church as ' The Body of Christ '
he was not using a metaphor. There were occasions when
he did use genuine metaphors—the Building or Temple,
and the Bride. But these two metaphors are far less
frequently used than is the phrase, ' The Body of Christ.'
And they are both subordinate to and understandable only
in terms of the Body.

' " Destroy this temple," said Jesus,[1] " and in three
days I will raise it up." Then said the Jews, " Forty and
six years was this temple in building, and wilt thou
rear it up in three days ? " But He spake of the temple
of His body.' The Building or the Temple always points
to the Body of Christ.

In Ephesians 2 : 20 Paul describes the Church as a
temple which is ' built upon the foundation of the apostles
and prophets, Jesus Christ Himself being the chief corner
stone.' But the architectural metaphor at once breaks down
when he goes on to speak of this building as one which
' *grows* into a holy temple in the Lord.' A building is built
—it does not grow. The word ' grow,' in this context,
points beyond the metaphor to the reality of the Church
as the Body of Christ.

Likewise the figure of the Bride of Christ derives its

[1] Jn. 2 : 19-21.

significance only from Christ's Body. This is the case not only when the Church is compared to a pure bride,[1] but also when she is contrasted with a harlot.[2] In Ephesians 5 a parallel is drawn between husbands and their wives on the one hand and Christ and His Church on the other hand. Husbands are commanded to love their wives as if they were their own *bodies*.[3] For Christ loves *His* Bride in the same way—'for we are members of His *body*, of His flesh and of His bones.'[4] The metaphor of the Bride is to be understood in terms of the reality of the Body.

When we turn to the Gospel narrative we find that the bodily relation between Christ and His Church is so clearly described that we are left in no doubt that both the architectural metaphor of the Building and the marriage metaphor of the Bride are quite inadequate to express its organic nature. To take but two examples.

Christ did not hesitate to liken His relationship with His people to that of the vine with its branches. One may say that a vine has no branches. The branches are themselves the vine. The whole emphasis of this discourse [5] is on the fact that the life of the vine *is* the life of the branches. The sap which flows through the vine is, at the same time, flowing through the branches. The fruit which the vine bears is, in fact, born by the branches. The relation of the one to the other is not only completely organic. It is a relation in which the vine is indistinguishable from the branches. They are identical.

Again. " Except ye eat the flesh of the Son of Man, and drink His blood, ye have no life in you."[6] So ' hard ' was this saying that ' from that time many of His disciples went back, and walked no more with Him.' The saying

---

[1] 2 Cor. 11 : 2 ; Eph. 5 : 25 ff.   [2] 1 Cor. 6 : 16.   [3] Eph. 5 : 28.
[4] Eph. 5 : 29-30.   [5] Jn. 15 : 1 ff.   [6] Jn. 6 : 53 ff.

divided disciples from fellow-travellers. It revealed the outlines of the Body. The word which the Authorised Version translates ' eat ' is a word which is normally used to describe the action of animals munching grass. This is no discreet swallowing of a wafer. It is a chewing, a munching of that which is uncompromisingly physical. According to Jesus, it is a chewing of His flesh. He could have used no more forthright language to emphasise the thoroughly organic relation which obtains between Him and His Church. His flesh was to become their flesh. His body was to become their body.

It is with these considerations in mind that we must discard the use of the word ' metaphor ' when applied to the phrase ' the Body of Christ.' For, in the words of the distinguished New Testament scholar J. A. T. Robinson, ' to say that the Church is the Body of Christ is no more of a metaphor than to say that the flesh of the incarnate Jesus . . . is the Body of Christ'.[1] Neither of them 'is "like" His Body (Paul never says this) : each of them *is* the Body of Christ, in that each of them is the physical complement and extension of the one and the same Person and Life.' [1]

Why, we may ask, does this conception of the Church as the Body of Christ play such a central part in the thought of Paul ? It was due, of course, in very large measure to his taking with the utmost seriousness not only the teaching of his Lord but also the whole movement of the Incarnation. But all this had leaped into life for him in his dramatic encounter with the risen Christ on the Damascus road. Paul had been persecuting the Church. He had ' made havoc of the Church, entering into every house, and haling men and women committed them to prison.' [2] Now he was on his way to Damascus and he

[1] *The Body*, S.C.M., 1952, p. 51.　　[2] Acts 8 : 3 ; cf. Gal. 1 : 13.

had one aim in view—to continue his persecution of the Church. And, on the road, ' suddenly there shined round about him a light from heaven : and he fell to the earth, and heard a voice saying unto him,' *not*, " Why persecutest thou *the Church* ? " but, " Why persecutest thou *Me* ? " And, lest he should be left in the slightest doubt as to whom he was, in fact, persecuting, the risen Christ continued, " I am Jesus *whom thou persecutest*." [1] That was to say that when Paul had stood, holding the coats of the men who were stoning Stephen,[2] he had witnessed the persecution of the Body of Christ. When he had made havoc of the Church he had made havoc of none other than Christ. When he had cast men and women into prison he had incarcerated Christ Himself. " Inasmuch as ye have done it unto one of the least of these my brethren, ye have done it unto me." [3] " Why persecutest thou *Me* ? " demanded Jesus. This was to say, in effect, " When you persecute the Church you are persecuting Me. I and My Church are *one*."

In the light of this experience, the seemingly extravagant language of Paul takes on the aspect of sober truth.

The sufferings of the Church are nothing less than the sufferings of Christ Himself. ' The sufferings of Christ abound in us.' [4] ' I fill up that which is behind of the afflictions of Christ in my flesh for His body's sake, which is the Church.' [5]

The Church possesses not only the attributes of Christ but also the fulness of Christ Himself. ' The Church . . . is His body, the *fulness* of Him that filleth all in all.' [6] But more than that. In Col. 2 : 9 Paul affirms that ' In Him (whose fulness fills the Church) dwelleth all the fulness of the *Godhead* bodily.' It therefore appears that, through

---

[1] Acts 9 : 3 ff.   [2] Acts 7 : 58.   [3] Mat. 25 : 40.   [4] 2 Cor. 1 : 5.   [5] Col. 1 : 24.   [6] Eph. 1 : 23.

Christ—and through Christ alone—the Church is partaker in the very life of the Trinity Himself.

As Christ is the sovereign Ruler of the world and is the Lord of life and of death, so is His Body, the Church ; for ' all things are yours ; whether . . . the world, or life, or death, or things present, or things to come; all are yours.' [1] Small wonder that, in this faith, Paul was able to affirm from his own personal experience—" I can do all things through Christ which strengtheneth me." [2] The explanation of his extraordinary life was the fact that he knew himself to be realistically united with, grafted into the Person of Jesus Christ. This faith he summed up in the otherwise inexplicable affirmation—" To me to live is Christ ! " [3]

It was because the Reformers took the Incarnation and the experience of the primitive Church with the greatest seriousness that they arrived at a much ' higher ' doctrine of the Church than is held by most of their successors to-day. Luther's position is crystal clear : Christ not only gives the Church ' all that is His ' ; He gives the Church ' His body and His very self.' [4] Calvin went so far as to insist that the body of Christ is so given to the Church that it is ' not so much His as ours.' [5] The contemporary resurgence of interest in the work of the Reformers and in Biblical theology as a whole is beginning to give the Protestant Church an ecclesiology which is much closer to the original Reformed position and much more faithful to the apostolic tradition than has been the case for centuries. Thus, Karl Ludwig Schmidt affirms, ' Christ is the ἐκκλησία itself.' [6] ' Ecclesiology and Christology are identical.' [7]

[1] 1 Cor. 3 : 21-23. [2] Phil. 4 : 13. [3] Phil. 1 : 21. [4] A Treatise on Christian Liberty, United Lutheran edition of works of Martin Luther, Vol. II, p. 320. [5] Inst. 4.17.3. [6] The Church, A. & C. Black, 1950, p. 16. [7] ibid. p. 21.

Oscar Cullmann holds that ' the resurrection body of Christ is identical with the Church.' [1] Dietrich Bonhoeffer is even more explicit, ' The fellowship of the baptised (is) a body which is identical with Christ's own Body. . . . Jesus Christ is at once Himself and His Church. . . .[2] Christ *is* the Church.' [3]

It is from this background that we may begin to understand that our Lord was not jesting when He affirmed that we could actually love as He has loved,[4] that we can do as He Himself has done,[5] and, more than that—that we can do even greater works than He has done.[6]

The Church is indeed the Body of Christ. ' All things *are* ours.' We possess His fulness—a fulness not only of knowing but of being. The Church receives not only Christ's benefits. The Church receives Christ Himself. The Church is partaker in His divine humanity, partaking ' so literally that all that happened in and through that Body in the flesh can be repeated in and through (the Church) now.' [7] The Christian and the Church have been united organically with Christ. They take into themselves the very life of Christ as ' new tissues take on the rhythms and metabolism of the body into which they have been grafted.' [8]

And nowhere is this central truth more clearly seen than when the Church gathers round the Table of her Lord.

In no other area of belief is Protestant thought more confused and more anæmic than in the doctrine of the Lord's Supper. It is here that men should see most vividly the real self-giving of Christ to His Church and the sub-

[1] *Early Christian Worship*, S.C.M., 1953, p. 18.   [2] *Cost of Discipleship*, S.C.M., 1951, p. 184.   [3] *Ibid.* p. 185.   [4] Jn. 13 : 34.   [5] Jn. 13 : 15.   [6] Jn. 14 : 12.   [7] J. A. T. Robinson, op. cit., p. 47.   [8] *ibid.*, p. 63.

stantial participation by the Church in His divine human-ity. In fact, there are few who see anything of the sort.

The Protestant confusion springs from a proper concern to oppose the Roman Catholic doctrine of transubstantia-tion. This important concern has to do, not with the question, ' Do we in fact receive the flesh and blood of Christ in the sacrament ? ' but with the quite subordinate question, ' Are the bread and wine in fact *changed* into the flesh and blood of Christ ? '

Around this secondary question the Reformers did battle not only with Rome but also with one another. Every shade of conviction is evident in the writings of the Reformers when this subordinate question is under debate. But there is almost complete unanimity upon the primary, the important and the neglected question as to whether we really *receive* the flesh and blood of Christ in the sacrament. Those who were most concerned to refute the Roman Catholic doctrine in the sixteenth century, were quite clear that the church does in fact receive the body and blood of her Lord. They could not deny it without denying the words and the actions of Christ—and this they had no intention of doing.

The wise rejection of the Roman Catholic doctrine of transubstantiation has led, in great areas of the Protestant church and especially in the minds of nearly all her laymen, to the tragic abandonment of the central truth of the whole mystery, so that, not only has the mode of operation been regarded as hocus pocus (*hoc est corpus meum*), but the un-speakable condescension of the Lord of the Church in giving the very substance of His life to His people has also been regarded as hocus pocus. The inevitable result has been that, when Christ's people gather around His table they do not *believe* that they receive His body and His blood. They believe that they receive bread and wine. Their faith has its reward. They *receive* bread and wine. They do *not* receive His body and His blood. The Church lives by faith. . . .

It is small wonder that the life of the Church is so often lacking in internal dynamic. Small wonder that she is so weak and lifeless,[1] a poor shadow of the life of her Saviour. In her concern to be truly ' spiritual ' on the one hand and ' rational ' on the other hand in her attitude to the Supper, the Church has become more ' spiritual ' and more ' rational ' than the Christ who gave her the sacrament. And in so doing the Church stands in peril of receiving little more than a ghostly wraith of the God whose intention was that His Body should throb with the life of His own divine humanity as the branches pulsate with the life of the vine.

Jesus sat at the table in the Upper Room. He took the bread in His hands and He said, " Take, eat : this is my body, which is broken for you." [2] The occasion was one of awful solemnity. Both He and His disciples knew that He was about to die. And, before He died, He was constituting them as His Church and giving them a kingdom [3] with all the powers of that Kingdom. This He did not merely by word but by a deed which was of such fundamental importance that He ordained that it should be continued without ceasing until His second coming in glory.[4] Until that day, the life of the Church was to be nourished by the life of Christ Himself in a manner at once spiritual and physical. It was to be sustained by His body. " Take, eat : this is my body."

It is generally agreed that the ' is ' means that the bread

[1] 1 Cor. 11 : 29 ff.   [2] 1 Cor. 11 : 24 ; cf. Mk. 14 : 22 ; Lu. 22 : 19 ; Mt. 26 : 26.   The words, ' This is my body,' occur in all four accounts.   [3] Lu. 22 : 29.   [4] 1 Cor. 11 : 26 ; cf. Lu. 22 : 30.

was in fact the body of Christ or else that it represented the body of Christ. It would seem that the latter interpretation is the more probable one when we consider the parallel saying of our Lord, " This cup is the new covenant in my blood." [1] The chalice was clearly not the new covenant although it certainly represented the new covenant. At all events, the question is a very secondary one, for whether the ἐστίν be translated ' is ' or ' represents,' our Lord was plainly saying that, in the Supper, He was giving His body and His blood to His Church. Whether the bread was itself the body of Christ or whether it was a sign of the body of Christ, the body of Christ *was* being given. A sign is that which points away from itself to something which really exists. It does not point to an illusion or a fiction. The bread does not represent a figment of the imagination. It represents a concrete reality. And it is the concrete reality of the body of Christ which the believer receives in the Supper.

On this basic question the Reformers[2] were all agreed. ' The sacrament,' wrote Luther, ' is the true body and blood of our Lord Jesus Christ under the bread and wine.' [3] The sacrament, ' is a divine sign, in which Christ's flesh and blood are truly present.' [4]

> *That we might never forget it*
> *Take my flesh, he said, and eat it,*
> *Hidden in this piece of bread*
> *Drink my blood in this wine, he said.*[5]

Calvin was no less explicit. ' The body which was once offered for our salvation, we are commanded to take and eat.'[6] ' There can be no falsehood or illusion in this word :

[1] Lu. 22 : 20, R.V.   [2] With the exception of Zwingli   [3] *Small Catechism,* Lenker edition, vol. 24, p. 28.   [4] *A Treatise Concerning the Blessed Sacrament and Concerning the Brotherhoods.* Works of Martin Luther. U.L. Press. Vol. 2, p. 20. [5] *Luther's Hymns.* Ed. Lambert, p. 103.   [6] Inst. 4 ; 17 ; 1.

" Take, eat, drink ; this is my body which is given for you ; this is my blood which is shed for the remission of sins." By commanding us to take, He signifies that He is ours ; by commanding us to eat and drink, He signifies that He is become *one substance* with us.'[1] ' Under the symbols of bread and wine, Christ is truly exhibited to us, even His body and blood . . . that being made partakers of His *substance*, we may experience His power.'[2] Nowhere does he express his position more simply and clearly than in his little book, ' Instruction in Faith,' written for the people of Geneva and published in 1537. Not only are the riches of Christ presented to us in the Supper, but, Calvin affirms, ' *Christ* with all His riches is there presented to us, not less than if He could be put in the presence of our eyes and be touched by our hands.'[3] So literal is our participation in the body and blood of Christ that Calvin finds in it the guarantee and ground of the immortality of our flesh—' He (Christ) not only brings there to our spirits assured confidence of eternal life, but also renders us certain of the immortality of our flesh. For our flesh is already vivified by Christ's immortal flesh.'[4]

Few congregations in Christendom were better informed on the Roman Catholic doctrine of transubstantiation and the Protestant doctrine of the Lord's Supper than that which gathered in the Kirk of Edinburgh in February 1589 to hear the now classic sermons of Robert Bruce on the theme of the Sacraments. To this critical congregation Bruce unfolded the biblical doctrine of the Lord's Supper. ' The true body and blood of Christ Jesus is . . . really present . . . in the Supper.'[5] ' Look how busy the Minister is in breaking that Bread, in pouring out that Wine, in giving that Bread and Wine to thee ; as busy is Christ in

[1] *Inst.* 4 ; 17 ; 3.   [2] *Inst.* 4 ; 17 ; 11.   [3] *Instruction in Faith* (1537), tr. Paul T. Fuhrmann, Lutterworth Press, 1949, p. 70.   [4] *ibid.* p. 70 ff.   [5] Robert Bruce's *Sermons on the Sacrament*. Laidlaw's trsltn., Oliphant, 1901, p. 129.

breaking His own body unto thee, and in giving thee the juice of His own body.'[1] 'If Christ be not both eaten and digested, He can do us no good.'[2] 'It is impossible that I can get . . . the virtue that flows out of Christ except I get the *substance*, that is—Himself first.'[3] Our zeal decays and our knowledge and light decay, he cries, for 'we have only played the counterfeit and defrauded our souls of the body and blood of Christ, and taken only the outward sacrament.'[4]

In his great sermon on "The Means of Grace," the founder of Methodism wrote, ''The cup of blessing which we bless, is it not the communion' or communication 'of the blood of Christ?''[5] And, in writing his hymns, Charles Wesley was no less explicit—

> *Jesu, Master of the Feast,*
> *The feast itself thou art,*[6]

and again

> *Now, Lord, on us thy flesh bestow,*
> *And let us drink thy blood,*
> *Till all our souls are filled, below*
> *With all the life of God.*[7]

In our own day, Karl Barth affirms that the elements are 'not merely . . . bread and wine but, without them therefore having altered their nature, . . . the body and blood of the Lord.' And he goes on to insist that this way of looking at the sacrament must not be regarded 'as less realistic' than that expressed in the Catholic doctrine of transubstantiation, or than that in the Lutheran doctrine of consubstantiation.'[8]

[1] op. cit. 32. [2] op. cit. 24. [3] op. cit. 11. [4] op. cit. 45. [5] Wesley's *Standard Sermons*. Vol. 1 ed. E H. Sugden Epnorth Press, 1921, p. 252 f (Wesley's italics). [6] *A Collection of Hymns for the use of the people called Methodists*. Wesleyan Conference Office, London, 1876. Hymn 905. [7] *Ibid*. Hymn 901. [8] *Church Dogmatics*, Eng. ed., 1 : 1 : 99.

In the Faith and Order volume *Intercommunion*, T. F. Torrance writes 'The church is given through the Eucharist a relation in being . . . to Christ. . . . The believing Church is given to step over the eschatological boundary and to partake of the divine nature.' [1]

Such language is faithful to the doctrine of the Reformers; it is faithful to the experience of the greatest saints of the Church; and it is faithful to the explicit affirmations of the Lord of the Church Himself. But more than this. It is faithful to the whole movement of divine grace in Jesus Christ. This movement, as we have sought to show, was one which involved the self-giving of Christ in such a way that His whole being—the unity of His body-soul—was *given* unreservedly to mankind. " This is my body broken for you. Take it. Eat it. He that eateth my flesh dwelleth in me and I in him."

The Church receives the very flesh and blood of Jesus Christ. She becomes nothing less than the Body of Christ. His life is her life. His nature is her nature. His being is her being. Christ is the Church.

[1] *Intercommunion*, ed. Baillie & Marsh, S.C.M., 1952, p. 335 ff.

CHAPTER THREE

THE HEAD OF THE BODY

THE CHURCH, we say, is the Body of Christ. At the same time, however, we also say—" Christ is the Head of the Body." [1] He stands over against the Church not only as Reconciler but also as Judge. The only standing ground which the Church possesses before Him is the standing ground of the man who will not lift up so much as his eyes unto heaven, but smites himself upon his breast and cries—" God be merciful to me a sinner ! " [2]

There is a strong element of truth in the contention that the Church is an extension of the Incarnation. But that Church which is *simply* an extension of the Incarnation is not the Church of Christ. Such a Church has no need to point beyond herself to her Lord. She is Christ in such a way that she need only point to herself. For her, the preaching of the Gospel is of minor importance. She sees the Sacraments in isolation from the Gospel because she believes that she is in a position to *dispense* the life of Christ without reference to any authority higher than herself.

The Church thus dethrones God. She becomes an idol. She takes on the aspect of a totalitarian state whose pretensions are frankly demonic. She is no longer Christ's servant. She is His patron.

Such an attitude is a far cry from that of the early

[1] cf. Col. 1 : 18, Eph. 4 : 15, 16 ; 5 : 23 ; 1 : 22, 23.   [2] Lu. 18 : 13.

Christians whose first confession of faith was " Jesus is
Lord ! " [1] They undoubtedly rejoiced in the fact that they
were the real Body of Christ. Yet they had no confidence
in themselves. Their sole confidence was in their Lord.
They knew that they could not stand in their own name
before God. Their trust was in the Mediator. Hence their
prayer was ever " through Jesus Christ our Lord."

The subordination of the Church to Christ is emphasised
by the plain fact that the Church is a sinful Church. The
Church which is ' simply ' an extension of the Incarnation
affirms its own sinlessness. Yet the sign of maturity in
the Christian Church, as in the Christian individual, is the
connection between growth in holiness and consciousness
of (although certainly not pre-occupation with) sin. In
one of his earlier letters Paul describes himself as ' the least
of the apostles.' [2] In a later epistle he has become ' less
than the least of all saints.' [3] And in a letter written towards
the close of his life he calls himself ' the chief of sinners.' [4]
As the Church becomes more holy she becomes more
conscious of sin. And the reason is not far to seek. Growth
in holiness comes when the eyes of the Church are fixed
upon her risen Lord. And when she dares to look at Him
she sees Him not only as Saviour and Sanctifier. She sees
Him also as Judge. If her eyes do not rise above herself
she sees Him neither as Saviour nor as Judge. And hence,
knowing no other judge than herself, she knows nothing
of her sin. But once her eyes rise up to meet her Lord's
eyes, she sees both His holiness and her own sin.[5] And if
the Body of Christ does not daily confess its sin, it becomes
a law unto itself. It fails to echo the cry of the Rock on
whom the Church was built—" Judgment must begin at
the house of God." [6] It exalts itself to God's throne. To

---

[1] 1 Cor. 12 : 3, A.R.S.V.   [2] 1 Cor. 15 : 9. About the year 56.   [3] Eph. 3: 8.
About the year 62.   [4] 1 Tim. 1 : 15. About the year 66.   [5] cf. Gen. 28 : 17;
Ex. 3 : 6; Isa. 6 : 5 ; Mat. 17 : 6; Lu 5 : 8.   [6] 1 Pet. 4 : 17.

such a proud, self-sufficient Church the voice of Jesus comes—" Thou sayest, ' I am rich and increased with goods and have need of nothing ; ' and knowest not that thou art wretched and miserable and poor and blind and naked. . . .[1] Thou hast a name that thou livest, and art dead ! " [2]

The Church, therefore, is not autonomous. The Church is not a democratic institution. Neither is she an autocratic society subordinate only to earthly rulers. She is entirely dependent on her Lord.

This fact is heavily underlined by three great historical events—the Ascension, Pentecost and the Second Coming of Christ. If the Church holds to the truth that she is the Body of Christ, and if, in *practice*, she rejects the truth that she is, at the same time, subject to Christ, then these three momentous events become quite irrelevant.

At Pentecost, the Spirit was sent to lead the Church into all the truth. But the Church now claims to be herself the Truth. She has no need of the Spirit. She is and has the Way, the Truth, and the Life, no man cometh unto the Father but by her. This is an inevitable consequence if the Church be purely and simply an extension of the Incarnation. She possesses all the power, all the inspiration, all the comfort that she needs. There is no authority higher than herself. Such a Church is seeking her *own* kingdom. She is, in fact, seeking herself. She does not seek in vain. She *finds* herself. She does not find God.

The Ascension and the Second Coming of Christ are the two supreme facts of history, the two bright beacons, by which the Church must steer her course on earth. These are the places where the divine and the human most evidently meet ; where eternity most plainly enters time ; where God in the flesh most visibly meets with man in the

[1] Rev. 3 : 17.   [2] Rev. 3: 1.

flesh. The Church must constantly look *back* for guidance to the concrete events in the life of her Lord—His Incarnation, His Crucifixion, His Resurrection—all of which are gathered up in His triumphant Ascension. She must constantly look *forward*, re-forming her life in expectation of His Second Coming. To refer once more to Peter, the Rock—'The day of the Lord will come as a thief in the night . . . (therefore) what manner of persons ought ye to be in all holy conversation and godliness, looking for and hasting unto the coming of the day of God.'[1]

If the Church, on her pilgrimage, turns her eyes from these two beacons, she will make shipwreck on the rocks of her own pride. If she looks for guidance to her own sinful nature she will be lost, and the very nature which she prized so much will vanish like a stream in the sands. For the nature of the Church, which is the nature of Jesus Christ Himself, is a *gift* of God. It is a gift which is given afresh every day; it is received only by humble faith. Like the manna which was given to Israel on her desert journey, it disintegrates if it is hoarded.[2] This gift is never *possessed* by the Church. It may not, as it were, be put in her pocket and forgotten until she thinks she needs it—like a book which is kept on a dusty shelf and pulled down when convenient; or a wafer locked away in a casket to be brought out when the Church sees fit and manipulated as she chooses. The nature of the Church is a gift from God which must be received afresh from moment to moment. It may be received, we say, only by faith. And the distinctive characteristic of *Christian* faith is that it is bound up inextricably with God's historic action in the Person of Jesus Christ.

The Church, let us repeat, *is* the glorious Body of

[1] 2 Pet. 3 : 10-12.   [2] Ex. 16 : 20.

Christ, partaker in His power, in His nature, in His life. She is a Body which rejoices in nothing more than in the absolute sovereignty of Him who is her Head.

It therefore appears that the Church's faith in her nature as the Body of Christ may have results which are either demonic or divine. Everything depends upon whether or not that faith is maintained along with an equally deep conviction that Christ is the *Head* of the Body. That is the crux of the matter.

Now, the ultimate reason which lies behind this conviction is the reason from which all other reasons derive their significance and their force. It is the belief that the One who called the Church into being was, and is, none other than the living God Himself. It is the belief that Christ is divine.[1]

There are few who will assert that this belief is so elementary as to be unworthy of our reflection. It is, to be sure, the first step in theology. It is also the last step of all. He who has never had honest doubts, who has never seriously questioned this basic affirmation, is unlikely to understand the nature of the Church or to have a realistic faith in Him who is the Church's Head. He may be competent to write perfectly orthodox theology. But until his breath has been taken away by the overwhelming force of this confession, and until he has seen something of the staggering implications of this claim, the Church will remain for him either an idol or a purely human institution, divorced from the living, active, ever-present God. He who says " Jesus is Lord " will be quite unaffected by his confession if he is yet uncertain who this Jesus is whom he addresses as Lord. It was for this reason that the great Assembly of Christian Churches meeting in Amsterdam

[1] Ro. 9 : 5.

in 1948 adopted as its basic confession of faith, not ' Jesus is Lord,' as had the early Church, but ' Jesus Christ is God and Saviour.' [1] By this they meant no more than the early Church had meant. But they made explicit what was implicit in the primitive confession. ' Jesus Christ is *God* . . .' But this raises that question which determines whether the Church is subject to herself or whether she is subject to the One who called her into being. It is the simple and the ultimate question regarding the truth of this confession. Was Christ, is Christ, in actual fact, divine? If He who founded the Church is not divine— and, in all seriousness, how sure are we that He is?—then the Church is a purely human institution answerable to herself alone. But if, and only if, Christ is divine, then the Church is, in the most absolute sense, wholly subject unto Him; He is her sovereign Lord.

In the first place, we must be quite clear about the fact that Christ Himself claimed to be divine. He made the claim in so many words and He made it in certain significant deeds.

Amongst the most important of the sayings of Jesus is the group of ' I ' sayings where the emphatic pronoun, ἐγώ, signifies the sovereign ' I '—' I and I alone,' ' none but I.' [2] Karl Ludwig Schmidt has underlined the importance of these sayings as emphasising Jesus' consciousness of His own divinity.[3] When, for example, He says, " If I (ἐγώ), with the finger of God, cast out devils . . ." [4] the ἐγώ makes it very plain that ' the finger of God ' is none other than the finger of the One to whom the ἐγώ refers. *Jesus*

---

[1] Man's *Disorder and God's Design. The First Assembly of the World Council of Churches*, Vol. 5, S.C.M., 1949, p. 9.   [2] cf. A. M. Hunter, *The Work and Words of Jesus*, S.C.M., 1950, p. 88.   [3] In *Le Problème du Christianisme primitif*, referred to by A. M. Hunter, *op. cit.*   [4] Lu. 11 : 20 ; cf. Mat. 12 : 28.

casts out devils. He does it with the finger of God. He claims that God's finger is *His* finger. It is not surprising that He was accused of blasphemy.

When Christ is speaking of the last days,[1] He declares —" But of that day and that hour knoweth no man, no, not the angels which are in heaven, neither the Son, but the Father." [2] No human being knows. But more—no, angel knows. But even more than that—not even *the Son* knows. Only the Father knows. Who, then, is this Son who is subordinate only to the Father? The context makes it very plain that Jesus is referring to none but Himself. Immediately before [3] this declaration and immediately after it [4] He refers to Himself as ' the Son.' Not even the most severe critic will argue that this ' the Son ' passage refers to a *different* Son. No : Jesus is here declaring Himself to be Son of God in a way which asserts His superiority not only to all mankind, but also to all the angels of heaven.

The time came in Christ's ministry when John's disciples came to Him asking precisely the question which we are considering.[5] And Jesus replied by pointing to the miracles which He had done ". . . the blind receive their sight . . . the lepers are cleansed . . . the dead are raised up . . . ;" and then He offered His great prayer of thanksgiving,[6] concluding with the words " All things are delivered unto Me of My Father. And no man knoweth the Son but the Father ; neither knoweth any man the Father save the Son, and he to whomsoever the Son will reveal Him." This particular saying of Jesus has been described as ' a bolt from the Johannine blue,' for the estimate which Jesus here sets on His own person could only be made by one who was conscious of being the

---

[1] Mk. 12 : 1-9. [2] Mk. 13 : 32. [3] Mk. 13 : 26 ; cf. 14 : 62. [4] Mk. 13 : 34. [5] Mat. 11 : 3. [6] Mat. 11 : 25 ff.

unique Son of God. He alone knows the Father. No man may come to know the Father except He, Jesus, chooses to make Him known. Here, Christ claims a position of unshared Sonship.

Christ's claim to be the unique Son of God is, however, made *explicit* both in private and in public. He seeks out the man whose sight He had restored and who had been excommunicated from the temple. He asks him—"Dost thou believe on the Son of God?"[1] "Who is He, Lord, that I might believe on Him?" And Jesus said unto him, "Thou has both seen Him, and it is He that talketh with thee." And the man worshipped Him.

On the night before His death, in the palace of the high priest, Jesus is asked point-blank "*Art* Thou the Christ, the Son of the Blessed?"[2] And back comes the unequivocal reply "I am!"[3] The next day His enemies mocked Him with the words "He trusted in God; let Him deliver Him now, if He will have Him: for *He said* 'I am the Son of God.'"[4]

It is, of course, possible to assert that, *all* men being sons of God, Jesus' claim was nothing more than a testimony to His kinship with His brethren, a frank affirmation of the brotherhood of man. One can make this assertion only by closing one's mind to the religio-social atmosphere in which Jesus lived, and by bringing Greek categories of thought to bear upon a purely Jewish situation. All Christ's adversaries believed themselves to be sons of God in a non-unique sense. They rebelled against Christ's claim because the unique nature of the Sonship which He claimed amounted, in their estimation, to nothing less than blasphemy. "He hath spoken

[1] Jn. 9: 35 ff. [2] 'The Blessed' is, of course, merely a Jewish reverential circumlocution to avoid speaking directly of God. [3] Mk. 14: 62. [4] Mat. 27: 43.

blasphemy ! [1] By our Law He ought to die because He made Himself the Son of God." [2] His blasphemy was nothing less than an unqualified claim to be divine. He was ' making Himself *equal* with God.' [3] That was His offence. That was the ultimate reason why the Jews sought to destroy Him, ". . . because that *Thou, being a man, makest Thyself God*." [4]

We turn now from the sayings of Jesus to consider those events which point most plainly to His claim to be divine. We do well to reflect on the significance of the Annunciation ; [5] the voice of God at the Baptism [6] and at the Transfiguration ; [7] and the divine intervention in the wilderness [8] and in the Garden of Gethsemane.[9] But here we are concerned, not with what *others* thought of Jesus, but with what Jesus thought of Himself. The Gospels are full of events in which Jesus' claim to divinity is implicit. We shall select only the two most significant.

First, we observe that Christ claimed to forgive men's sins. He turns to the woman who ' was a sinner ' and He says, "Thy sins are forgiven." [10] He turns to the man who was sick of the palsy and He says, " Son, thy sins be forgiven thee." [11] And how right the scribes and Pharisees were ' to say within themselves, Who is this that forgiveth sins also ? [12] Who can forgive sins but God only ? ' [13] They state the problem precisely. None but God can forgive men's sins. And Jesus makes this claim for Himself. He claims that He is competent to do what God alone can do ; He claims that He is able to meet the ultimate need of all mankind—the need for the

[1] Mat. 26 : 65. [2] Jn. 19 : 7 ; cf. Lev. 24 : 16 ; Jn. 10 : 36. [3] Jn. 5 : 18. [4] Jn. 10 : 33. [5] Lu. 1 : 26-38. [6] Mk. 1 : 11. [7] Mat. 17 : 5. [8] Mk. 1 : 13. [9] Lu. 22 : 43. [10] Lu. 7 : 48. [11] Mk. 2 : 5. [12] Lu. 7 : 49. [13] Mk. 2 : 7.

51

forgiveness of sin. " Why doth this man thus speak blasphemies ? " [1]

But Christ's claim to be divine becomes quite unmistakable on the night of the Last Supper. The claim is made in a manner which no Jew could regard as being ambiguous.

The pride of Israel had always been that they were the people with whom God had made a Covenant. He had chosen them and bound them to Himself by this solemn bond. But for centuries Israel had looked expectantly into the future knowing that God would bring to them a new and a better day. For He had promised that it would be so. He had promised them a *New* Covenant, " Behold the days come that . . . I will make a new covenant with the house of Israel . . ." [2] This Covenant was to be made by a direct act of God. For God *alone* could make such a Covenant.

And yet—with the shadow of the Cross upon Him, Jesus gathers His disciples (the remnant of Israel, we may say) in an upper room. And there He breaks bread, saying —" This is My body " ; and He takes the cup and utters the words for which Israel has waited so long—" This cup is the *new covenant* in my blood." [3] The New Covenant ! At last the hope of Israel was realised. God had fulfilled His promise. *God* had fulfilled His promise ! The same Word who had come to Jeremiah long ago now took His stand amongst His people as the Word made flesh declaring the fulfilment of His promise. Jesus had done what God alone could do—established the New Covenant.

The claim to be the unique Son of God, the claim to forgive men's sins, the claim to fulfil the divine promise to Israel by Himself establishing the New Covenant—all

[1] Mk. 2 : 7.   [2] Jer. 31 : 31.   [3] 1 Cor. 11 : 25, A.R.S.V. ; cf. Mk. 14 : 24.

these facts point to Christ's own conviction that He was nothing less than divine. The claim is all the more powerful and convincing by reason of the fact that men are not urged to believe that it is true. It is something which is simply taken for granted by Jesus. It is self-evident. It is the fundamental pre-supposition of all that He says and does. It is implicit in every aspect of His ministry. Only rarely does it become explicit. But, on these rare occasions, we are left in no manner of doubt as to *Jesus'* estimate of His own nature.

" If ye had known Me, ye should have known My Father also." [1] " He that receiveth Me, receiveth Him that sent me." [2] To know Christ is to know God. To receive Christ is to receive God. Christ is one with the Creator. " I and My Father are one." [3]

We have seen that Jesus had no doubts concerning the fact of His divinity. But, inevitably, the question must arise—" Was He right ? "

In seeking an answer to that question we shall need to consider certain historical events ; but it is important to emphasise the fact that it would be both presumptuous and foolish if we were to base our answer on nothing greater than historical events and logical argument. To do so would be to subordinate God to our own interpretation of history and to our own frail logic. If Christ is divine, His divinity will only be demonstrated to men in any final sense by a direct revelation from the side of God Himself. Historical facts cannot, of themselves, prove the reality of the eternal. But historical facts, when illumined by the Spirit of God, can and do become the means whereby God is perceived. The Spirit is primary. But the Spirit does not work in a vacuum. He lays hold on history and makes

[1] Jn. 14 : 7.   [2] Mat. 10 : 40 ; cf. Jn. 13 : 20 ; 12 : 49.   [3] Jn. 10 : 30.

it speak of God. And, in the matter of the divinity of Jesus, the supreme event to which the Spirit points is Christ's resurrection from the dead.[1]

The significance of the Resurrection lies in the fact that it was *Christ* who was risen from the dead. It was the Christ who had said—" I am the Son of God. I and My Father are one." Had the life of Jesus ended on the Cross, men might be justified in suspecting that His claims to be divine had been no more than a grand illusion. But now, by the resurrection from the dead, Christ's pre-resurrection claims acquire a character and a force which they never had before. If His vision and His knowledge had been limited before the resurrection, they are not so limited now. Now, during the forty days, His great concern is not to offer His followers a new metaphysic; it is to impress upon them the significance of all He had done and said during His earlier ministry, " These are the words which I spake unto you whilst I was yet with you . . ."[2] Far from correcting the estimate which the disciples had made of His Person—" Thou art the Son of God ! "[3]—He does everything He can to confirm it. He claims all power in heaven and on earth.[4] He accepts the *worship* of the women on the road.[5] He accepts the confession " My Lord and my God ! "[6] Because of the Resurrection, every word and deed of Jesus which had pointed to His divinity is now endorsed as the word and deed of God.

It is, therefore, because of His Resurrection that Christ appears in a fundamentally different light from other men. There are very few things which all men have in common, but one such thing is the certainty of death. If a man rise from the dead to die no more, his resurrection proclaims

[1] Ro. 1 : 4.　　[2] Lu. 24 : 44 ff; cf. 24 : 25-27; Acts 1 : 2, 3.　　[3] Mat. 14 : 33.　cf. Mat. 16 : 16.　　[4] Mat. 28 : 18.　　[5] Mat. 28 : 9.　　[6] Jn. 20 : 28.

him the possessor of a nature higher than our own. His is a nature which prevents his being held by death. Life itself is in his power. Now we know of One alone who has the last say where death is concerned. That One is God Himself. And *Christ* had the last say where death was concerned. Life itself was in *His* power. Hence, through the Spirit, the believer perceives that it is by Christ's Resurrection that His divinity is most plainly proclaimed.

We do well, at this point, to recall the mass of objective evidence which, when illumined by the Holy Spirit, points to the historicity of the Resurrection. Such evidence is direct and indirect.

In the first place, the obvious direct evidence consists in the resurrection appearances to the disciples.

The women fled from a tomb that was *empty*.[1] And, on the road, they met Jesus face to face. They worshipped Him, received His command, and carried His message to the eleven. On the Emmaus road, the two disciples encountered Jesus, they were instructed by Him, they broke bread with Him in their village home, and they recognised Him before He left them.[2] Christ's first appearance to all the disciples[3] was in the upper room in Jerusalem where He gave them His blessing, partook of a common meal with them, and taught them from the Scriptures. This was only the beginning of many appearances before Christ ascended into heaven. He was seen by Peter. He was seen by the Twelve. He was seen by more than five hundred of the brethren at once.[4] But not only was He *seen*. He spent many days in the company of His followers —in Jerusalem,[5] in the surrounding villages,[6] in the

[1] Mat. 28 : 6 ff.　[2] Lu. 24 : 13 ff; cf. Mk. 16 : 12.　[3] Lu. 24 : 36 ff; cf. Mk. 16 : 14.　[4] Lu. 24 : 34; I Cor. 15 : 5 ff.　[5] Jn. 20 : 19 ff; Lu. 24 : 36 ff.　[6] Lu. 24 : 30.

countryside,[1] and by the Sea of Tiberias.[2] In other words, ' He showed Himself alive . . . by many infallible proofs, being seen of them forty days, and speaking of the things pertaining to the Kingdom of God.' [3]

It is significant that this direct evidence is found in all four Gospels, in the book of Acts and in the letters of Paul. It is, of course, possible to dismiss this evidence as being a later insertion of the early Church into the record. But one must have adequate grounds for adopting such a position. The vast majority of Christian and non-Christian scholars accept all the material to which reference has been made.

But if the direct evidence is strong, the indirect evidence is stronger still. Here the question, however remote, of a falsification of the record does not arise. We are dealing not so much with texts as with general attitudes and with the characters of men and groups to which an abundance of early non-Christian literature [4] bears witness. It all points to the fact of the Resurrection. To think oneself, soberly and realistically, into the situation of the first disciples is to discover a cumulative weight of evidence which points with irresistible force to the reality of the Resurrection.

The first and the most obvious factor is the revolutionary change in the disciples on the first Easter Sunday. On the morning of that eventful day they were clearly broken, disillusioned men. They were in no mood to *imagine* the Resurrection, as some critics suggest. They had lost faith in themselves, for they had betrayed their cause. And they had lost faith in their Lord [5] as well, " We *had* hoped that He was the one to redeem Israel." [6] Despair had so taken

---

[1] Acts, 1 : 12. [2] Jn. 21 : 12. [3] Acts 1 : 3 ; cf. 10 : 41 ; 13 : 30.
[4] e.g. Pliny's letters to Trajan ; Josephus, *Antiquities*. 18.3.3. [5] Mk. 16 : 11.
[6] Lu. 24 : 21 A.R.S.V.

hold of them that, when the women brought the news from the empty tomb, they flatly refused to believe them. ' Their words seemed to them as idle tales, and they believed them not.' [1] The possibility that they would ever see Christ again was so far removed from their minds that when He did appear to them they did not even recognise Him. Mary mistook Him for the gardener.[2] Two other disciples asked Him " Art thou only a stranger in Jerusalem?" [3] He came to the eleven in the upper room and they thought they were looking at a ghost.[4]

Such was their mood on the first day of the week. A mood of confused hopelessness and of bitter disillusionment. They hid themselves away behind locked doors in an obscure room in Jerusalem, ' for fear of the Jews.' [5]

And then, miraculously, they become new men ! [6] They are no longer frightened fugitives. They are men of authority and power. We see them standing before a vast multitude of three thousand Jews in the city square, boldly accusing them of their guilt in crucifying Christ.[7] Folk speak of these once hopeless men as ' these that have turned the world upside down ! ' And the disciples give one reason for the transformation—' the resurrection of the Lord Jesus.' [8] " This Jesus hath God raised up, whereof we all are witnesses ! " [9] That was the reason which the disciples gave. It is hard to find an alternative explanation.

The Church chose the *first* day of the week as a special day for worship.[10] But God had set aside the *last* day of the week to be kept especially holy. On what grounds did

[1] Lu. 24 : 11 ; cf. Mk. 16 : 11.　[2] Jn. 20 : 15.　[3] Lu. 24 : 18.　[4] Lu. 24 : 37.　[5] Jn. 20 : 19.　[6] Lu. 24 ; cf. vv 41, 52.　[7] Acts 2 : 41, 36. [8] Acts 4 : 33.　[9] Acts 2 : 32 ; cf. 1 : 22 ; 2 : 24 ; 3 : 15, 26 ; 4 : 10, etc. [10] Acts 20 : 7 ; 1 Cor. 16 : 2 ; Rev. 1 : 10 ; *Didache* 14 : 1 ; Justin, *Apol.* 1 ; 67 : 3.

the Church change the last to the first ? Was it not because
it seemed most fitting to hold the highest festival on that
day of the week on which Jesus rose from the dead ? It
was on the first day of the week that Mary met Jesus at
the sepulchre.[1] It was on the first day of the week that
He met the disciples on the Emmaus road.[2] It was on the
first day of the week that He appeared to the eleven in
Jerusalem.[3] In six days God had made the heavens and
the earth and had ordained the seventh day to be a Sabbath
for His people. But something even greater than the first
creation had happened now. God had *rested* on the seventh
day. But He had *risen* on the first. What could His people
do but offer Him their special praise on this Easter
day ? This day spoke, with particular distinctness, of
the new creation and of the ultimate triumph of God.
Hence, it was the great day of worship—the day of the
Resurrection.

Why the sense of ' exuberant joy '[4] whenever men
partook of the Lord's Supper ? It was certainly not
primarily because men were recalling ' the Lord's *death* till
He came.' ' In the blinding light of the resurrection,' as
Oscar Cullmann points out, ' the thought . . . (of the) death
of Christ fell completely into the background.'[5] It was 'the
remembrance of those other occasions where Jesus,
immediately after His resurrection, appeared to the
disciples, while they were having a meal '[6] which made
the Eucharist such a joyous occasion.

If this were not the reason for their joy, we must ask
what the reason was. The Church's thankful pre-occupation
with the fact of Christ's risen presence at the feast was
emphasised by the eucharistic prayer, " Maranatha—

[1] Mat. 28 : 1; Mk. 16 : 2, 9.   [2] Lu. 24 : 13.   [3] Lu. 24 : 33, 36; cf. Jn. 20 : 19.
[4] Acts 2 : 46; cf. O. Cullmann, *Early Christian Worship*, tr. A. S. Todd &
J. B. Torrance, S.C.M., 1953, p. 15.   [5] *ibid*. p. 18.   [6] *ibid*. p. 15.

Come, Lord Jesus ! "[1] by the earliest confession of faith,
" Jesus *is* Lord," and by the present tense in the oldest,
Christian hymns, "Worthy *is* the Lamb that was
slain . . ."[2] The early Christian community rejoiced at its
worship because it believed that ' the Lamb that was slain '
had demonstrated the *fact* of His ' Power . . . and honour
and glory ' by His resurrection from the dead.

If the Resurrection were not an historical fact we are
confronted with a psychological problem of the first
magnitude. We have to account for the facts that the
Gospels are at one in recording the post-resurrection
appearances of Jesus ; that Luke, ' the beloved physician,'
who paid such scrupulous attention to detail,[3] describes a
Church which claimed to be, and acted precisely as though
it was, overwhelmed by the fact of the Resurrection ; and
that the Lord's Day, the Eucharist, the prayers, the hymns
and the confession of the early Church all speak with one
voice of the reality of the Resurrection and of its centrality
in the minds of the worshippers.

Thus far the historical material takes us. But it is not
far enough.

However impressive the objective evidence for the
divinity of Christ may be, it all remains in the realm of
the impersonal and the ultimately irrelevant [4] until it is
subjectively appropriated. This subjective appropriation
is, as we have already insisted, the work of the Holy Spirit.
He alone opens men's hearts and minds that the impossible
possibility may happen ; namely, that they may meet with
Christ and thereby know Him to be God.

It is true that, in a sense, this ' meeting ' itself comes

---

[1] I Cor. 16 : 22 ; cf. Rev. 22 : 20, for the Greek translation.   [2] Rev. 5 :
12 ; cf. 5 : 9, 13 ; 12 : 10-12 ; 19 : 1, 2, 6.   [3] Lu. 1 : 1-4.   [4] Lu. 16 : 31.

under the heading of ' objective' testimony. When men of every age and race and class and culture affirm that God in Christ has found them, that they have come to *know* Him as Lord, it is possible to claim that they are *wrong*. But it is not possible to claim that they do not *believe* that they know God in Christ. Their belief demands explanation. And, hence, it is added to the great weight of objective evidence.

But, again, we must say that, however impressive that evidence may be, it is insufficient without the inward testimony of the Holy Spirit. And His testimony is one which cannot be analysed or explained. It can only be experienced.

*　　*　　*

We have seen that the Resurrection of Jesus Christ and the testimony of the Holy Spirit left the Church in no doubt that Christ was none other than God. This meant that, knowing Him to be risen, the Church was not abroad in the world at her own charges. The Body of Christ was under orders from Him who was the *Head* of the Body.

And this was not only the *theology* which conditioned the disciples' thinking. It was the supreme reality which directed their lives. ' They were not only proclaiming the Resurrection as a fact,' writes J. S. Stewart,[1] '*they were living in it* as in a new country.' They knew that all their endeavours were entirely dependent upon the personal presence of their Lord. It was for this reason that they described that which had happened in the last three years as ' all that Jesus *began* both to do and teach.'[2] The book of the Acts of the Apostles was the record of all that Jesus *continued* both to do and teach. As Mark's Gospel has it,

[1] *A Faith to Proclaim*, Hodder & Stoughton, 1953, p. 109.　　[2] Acts 1: 1.

the disciples 'went forth, and preached every where, *the Lord working with them.*' [1]

The extraordinary results of their earliest activities—the multitudes which thronged into the Church,[2] the miracles of healing,[3] of judgment,[4] of release [5]—these they believed to be occasioned by no power of their own. They attributed everything to the activity of the Lord of the Church ' working with them.' " Ye men of Israel, why marvel ye at this," cried Peter, " as though by our *own* power we had made this man to walk . . . ? " He insisted that it was the power of the risen Lord which had healed the congenital cripple.[6] When the rulers of the people confronted the disciples with the question "By what power . . . have ye done this ? " they did not hesitate to affirm that all that they did was done by the power of " Jesus Christ . . . whom God raised from the dead ! " [7]

At each turning point in the swiftly developing life of the Church it is the risen Christ who is represented as intervening and directing His people into the way of *His* purpose.

When Peter, ' the rock,' was determined to restrict the Gospel to the children of Israel,[8] the Lord of the Church convinced him by word and by dramatic deed [9] that the Gospel was to be preached to *all* men. If the decision had been left to Peter, no Gentile converts would have been made. But the decision was taken by the Lord of the Church and " What was I," asked Peter, " that I could withstand God ? " [10]

At the height of Herod's persecution of the Church,[11] James the brother of John was killed, Peter himself was cast into prison, and the whole Church was dismayed at

[1] Mk. 16 : 20. [2] Acts 2 : 41 ; 4 : 4. [3] Acts 3 : 7. [4] Acts 5 : 5, 10.
[5] Acts 12 : 7 ff. [6] Acts 3 : 12 ff ; cf. Mat. 17 : 16 ff. [7] Acts 4 : 7-10.
[8] Acts 10 : 28 ; cf. 11 : 3. [9] Acts 10 : 44-46. [10] Acts 11 : 17. [11] Acts 12 : 1 ff.

the loss of two of its greatest leaders. At this critical juncture, Peter was delivered from his bonds by Christ's direct intervention. Neither guards, chains, keepers or gates could prevent his escape. Peter, whose part in the drama had been entirely passive, returned to the waiting Church declaring 'how *the Lord* had brought him out of the prison.'[1]

When Philip preached the Gospel to the Samaritans,[2] his ministry was attended with dramatic results. Multitudes believed and multitudes were healed. 'There was great joy in that city.' But, at the height of his success, the Lord of the Church intervened and commanded him to go out into the desert! 'And he arose and went.' The result was the conversion of one of the highest officials in the Ethiopian court. Thus the Gospel was carried to East Africa, and the Ethiopian Church took root.

When the first Christian missionaries would have continued their fruitful work in Asia Minor[3] they became convinced that, contrary to their own desire, they must turn their backs on this mission field, they 'were forbidden of the Holy Ghost to preach the word in Asia . . ., they assayed to go into Bithynia, but the Spirit suffered them not.'[4] Instead, they were directed to cross the seas and sail for Macedonia. And this they did, 'assuredly gathering that *the Lord* had called' them. And thus the Gospel reached the shores of Europe.

Paul insists that it was only by the command of Christ that he undertook his journey to Rome. [5] And, despite all manner of temporal set-backs—the rage of mobs who would have pulled him in pieces, [6] the schemes of fanatical Jews under oath to take his life,[7] and one of the most hazardous voyages recorded in the literature of the

---

[1] Acts 12 : 17.　　[2] Acts 8 : 5 ff.　　[3] Acts 16 : 5 ff.　　[4] Acts 16 : 6 ff; cf. 13 : 2.　　[5] Acts 23 : 11 ; cf. 27 : 23, 24.　　[6] Acts 23 : 10.　　[7] Acts 23 : 12.

sea [1]—it was to Rome that Paul eventually came. Thus, not only was the Church's greatest missionary planted in the heart of the Roman Empire but the Gospel which he carried was proclaimed in the very household of Caesar himself.[2]

And, according to those who were engaged in the work, all this was accomplished only because Christ was the living *Lord* of His Church. The Church moved like an inspired army because her life was governed by the ascended Christ. Hence, the thought of the early Church was dominated by a sense of the lordly rule of Christ. In his vision, the Christ whom the first Christian martyr saw was the Christ who was *regnant* over history.[3] And the Christ of John's vision on the isle of Patmos was the Christ who held the life of the Churches in His hand,[4] the Christ who sat upon the throne,[5] the Christ in whose praise the hymn was sung— " Alleluia ! For *the Lord God Omnipotent* reigneth ! " [6]

When the first disciples recovered from the initial shock of knowing that the faltering faith which they had mustered during their apprenticeship had been overwhelmingly justified and that Christ was indeed divine, they were thoroughly realistic in their recognition of the fact that His Godhead was no partial or subordinate Godhead. They were driven to the inescapable conclusion that He was, without qualification, ' our great God.' [7]

This meant that the Christ who had been their intimate companion was, in sober truth, none other than the Creator of the ends of the earth. That was what His divinity meant—either that or nothing at all.[8] They expressed their new-found knowledge in no uncertain way " All things

[1] Acts 27 : 14 ff. [2] Acts 27 : 24 ; Phil. 1 : 13, 4 : 22. [3] Acts 7 : 56. [4] Rev. 1 : 20 ; cf. 2 : 5. [5] Rev. 5 : 13. [6] Rev. 19 : 6. [7] Tit. 2 : 13, A.R.S.V. [8] cf. " Before Abraham was, I am." (Jn. 8 : 58) : also the note of pre-existence in the " I came forth . . ." sayings. (Jn. 16 : 28 ; 8 : 42, etc.).

were made by *Him* and without Him was not any thing made that was made."[1] "By *Him* were all things created, that are in heaven and that are in earth, visible and invisible . . . all things were created by Him and for Him : and He is before all things, and by Him all things consist."[2]

They knew that—*now*, in their present moment—the whole universe was under His control. . . . " All power is given unto Me in heaven and in earth."[3] And this knowledge was the source of their unshakable faith in the ultimate triumph of their Lord. ' The Kingdoms of this world' would, in fact, ' become the Kingdoms of our Lord.'[4] The day would come when ' at the name of Jesus, *every* knee should bow, of things in heaven and things in earth and things under the earth : and that every tongue should confess that Jesus Christ is Lord.'[5]

Hence, although they knew themselves to be Christ's Body, endued with His power and with His authority, they also knew, at the same time, that they were utterly dependent upon Him who was their Lord. These were the two great marks of the early Church. And it is clear that the first gained its reality from the second. The Church was partaker in the nature of her Lord. That was true only because her *whole* life, from moment to moment, was a gracious gift from Christ. He was Lord of her life in such a way as to exclude all other lords.[6] His sovereignty extended into every aspect of her being. That was what it meant for Him to be ' Lord.'

It was for this reason that the Church in the Acts did not guide herself so much by the teaching of the Lord. She allowed *the Lord* to guide her. She did not depend for her life so much upon what Jesus had done as upon what He was *doing* in her midst. She was less con-

---

[1] Jn. 1 : 3.　　[2] Col. 1 : 16, 17, cf. Eph. 1 : 20-23, 10.　　[3] Mat. 28 : 18 ;　　[4] Rev. 11 : 15.　　[5] Phil. 2 : 10-12.　　[6] cf. Karl Barth, *Credo*, Hodder & Stoughton, 1936, p. 51.

cerned with the doctrine that the Lord had risen than with her present experience of the fact that the Lord *was* risen.

In every age, this Christ-conscious Church knows that she is not an end in herself. She is *God's* means to *His* end. And she is the Body of Christ only when she serves that end. She is *able* to serve that end because she is, in fact, Christ's Body. She is Christ's Body only because she is wholly dependent upon Him.

Therefore, her confession of faith is always " *Jesus* is Lord." Her very life is dependent on the answer to her prayer—" Maranatha ! Come, Lord Jesus ! "

CHAPTER FOUR

A SPIRITUAL BODY

THIS CHURCH which is both subject to Christ's Lordship and also partaker in His nature is often described as ' a *spiritual* Body.' [1]

But it is precisely at the point where the word ' spiritual ' makes its appearance that many contemporary Christians think that they have entered the realm of unreality, of other-worldliness, and, therefore, of irrelevance. " If the Church be only the ' spiritual ' Body of Christ," they say, " she is not really the Body of Christ at all." Or, at least, she is the Body of Christ in such a way as has nothing to do with the hard facts of life, nothing to do with man as he is in all his material, flesh and blood reality. " If Christ be received . . . only by the Spirit and by faith then He is not received but by way of imagination, conceit and fantasy." Thus spoke the Roman priests to Robert Bruce in 1589.[2] And thus speak the great mass of men both inside and outside the Church to-day. Their speech may have its roots in the thought of ancient Greece, of Gautama Buddha, or of classical Hinduism. But it does not have its roots in the New Testament.

That which was spiritual for the ancient Greek was ultimately divorced from the material world. The ' spiritual ' for the Buddhist is escape from life in the world ; it is perfect detachment from the historical process so that he

---

[1] cf. 1 Cor. 15 : 44 ; 1 Pet. 2 : 5. [2] *Robert Bruce*, op. cit., p. 82.

who has reached perfection affirms, " Decay is inherent in all things that have come into being ; "[1] he has become an Ararat, he is free from all desire, his appetite for life-in-this-world has gone. Hindu spirituality is deliverance from the body, from material existence ; the spiritual man is the one who knows that the world and all things in it are illusion.

Such conceptions of the nature of ' spiritual ' must lead ultimately to a lack of social concern and a denial of the importance of men's bodies. For this reason, it is not easy to see how such a conception could have arisen within the Christian community which believed that it was *God* who had made this material world and all that is in it,[2] and that it was *God* who took our human flesh, who walked the roads of Palestine, who went about healing the bodies of men, who suffered and died and rose again with a Body which men saw and handled and felt. Yet such a conception seems to have arisen even in the early Church.

The Church at Corinth had a ' spirituality ' which appeared to have run wild. So ' spiritual ' was it, so unrelated to men's physical, moral and intellectual activities, so other-worldly was it that it mattered little if no-one understood the noise of many Christians speaking in unknown tongues in the Church.[3] It mattered little that there was fornication in the Church.[4] It mattered little that Christians were drunk at the Lord's Supper.[5] Such things as fornication and drunkenness had to do with the coarse, material world—they did not belong to the exalted world of the ' spirit.' These men—fornicators and drunkards though they were—were ' spiritual ' ! The body mattered nothing !

[1] Said to be the last words of Gautama Buddha. cf. Allan Menzies, *History of Religion*, Murray, 1911, p. 360.   [2] cf. 1 Tim. 4 : 4.   [3] 1 Cor. 14 : 9.   [4] 1 Cor. 5 : 1 ; 6 : 13, 15, 18.   [5] 1 Cor. 11 : 21.

To meet this situation, Paul gave the Corinthian believers a test whereby they might recognise that spirituality which was distinctively Christian. 'Now concerning spiritual gifts, brethren, I do not want you to be uninformed. You know that when you were heathen, you were led astray . . . Therefore I want you to understand that . . . no one can say "Jesus is Lord" except by the Holy Spirit.' [1] The test had its roots in the incarnate Son of God. The test was not the confession that " Christ is Lord "—there was always the danger that ' The Christ idea ' might be Lord. The test was the confession that "Jesus," born of Mary, lain in a manger, skilled as a craftsman, nailed to a cross, and physically risen from the dead—the test was the confession that " Jesus is Lord." The man who could sincerely make that confession was a man who was enlightened by the *Holy* Spirit. He alone was truly spiritual who acknowledged that the God who had taken human form, and had thereby made sacred the bodies of men, was the Lord of his life, of his mind and of his body. This was the Christian meaning of ' spiritual.'

Likewise, John saw the need for a definition and for a test of Christian spirituality. He opposed any notion of the ' spiritual ' which was not fully explicable in terms of the Incarnation. " Hereby know ye the Spirit of God," he declared. " Every spirit that confesseth that Jesus Christ is come in the flesh is of God. And every spirit that confesseth not that Jesus Christ is come in the flesh is not of God ; and this is that spirit of antichrist." [2] That is to say : that which is spiritual in a Christian sense is that which can only be understood and appropriated in terms of the physical Person of Jesus Christ. Not, be it noted, in terms of the attributes of Jesus Christ—His love, His spirit of forgiveness, His self-emptying—but in terms of

[1] 1 Cor. 12 : 1-4 A.R.S.V.   [2] 1 Jn. 4 : 2 ; cf. 4 : 15.

the physical Person of Jesus Christ. " Jesus Christ is come in the flesh." It is possible for us to use, to abuse, to possess an attribute. Not so with the physical Person of Christ. *He* remains Lord. And it is *He* who is the Lord of that which is spiritual.[1]

It need hardly be said that both Paul and John derived their conception of the nature of ' spiritual ' from none other than Jesus Himself. His conception is evident both in His teaching and in the great events of His life. Thus, His birth was the work of the Spirit.[2] His baptism was a baptism with the Spirit.[3] His sojourn in the wilderness was initiated by the Spirit.[4] His preaching was inspired by the Spirit.[5] His physical resurrection was effected by the Spirit.[6] But His conception of the nature of the ' spiritual ' is made explicit in a crucial discourse (Jn. 3 : 5-8) in which He is speaking of His own nature and also of the nature of those who believe in Him. " Except a man be born of water and of the Spirit, he cannot enter into the Kingdom of God. That which is born of the flesh is flesh ; and that which is born of the Spirit is spirit." That which is born of the Spirit is spirit. Our minds go back to the accounts of the conception of Jesus—" That which is conceived in her is of the Holy Ghost." [7] Nothing could be plainer than the fact that Jesus was born of the flesh of Mary. He was flesh. He was bone of our bone and flesh of our flesh. And, again, nothing could be plainer than the fact that He was born of the Spirit. He was spirit. That which is born of the Spirit is spirit. If we would know what ' spirit ' and ' spiritual ' mean we must look at Jesus Christ who is come in the flesh. And, looking at Him, we are forced to the conclusion that the ' spiritual ' is as material as the incarnate Christ.[8] A truly Christian spirituality has its centre in His

[1] 2 Cor. 3 : 17 ff.   [2] Lu. 1 : 35.   [3] Mat. 3 : 16.   [4] Mat. 4 : 1.   [5] Lu. 4 : 18.   [6] Ro. 8 : 11.   [7] Mat. 1 : 20. A.R.S.V.   [8] cf. 2 Cor. 5 : 17 ; 1 Sa. 10 : 6.

Person. It finds all its meaning in Him. It cannot go beyond Him. We may say that that which distinguishes the Christian conception of Spirit from all other conceptions of spirit lies in this : the Spirit is the Spirit of the Son—the physical, personal Son. The content of Christian experience of the ' spiritual ' is Jesus Christ Himself in all the fulness of His personal Presence. It is not an other-worldly spirituality. It is *Christ*. It is not a ' spiritualised ' Christ. There is but one Jesus Christ—and He is a Person of flesh and blood. The only Jesus Christ whom we know is the Risen One who said to Thomas, " Reach hither thy finger, and behold my hands, and reach hither thy hand and thrust it into my side."[1] That which is spiritual for the Christian and for the Church is that which has its roots and its meaning in the Person of the Incarnate Christ.

It is for this reason that we must now concentrate our gaze on the ' spiritual Body of Christ,' not so much as He meets us in the writings of Paul but as He meets us in the Evangelists' accounts of the historical deeds of this ' spiritual Body ' during the forty days that He walked the earth before He ascended into heaven. What was the nature of this Body ?

Here we are confronted with the inescapable historical fact that the spiritual Body was no phantom but was physical, material, flesh and blood. The disciples ' were terrified and affrighted and supposed that they had seen a spirit. And He said unto them, " Behold My hands and my feet that it is I myself ; *handle* Me and see, for a spirit hath not flesh and bones as ye see Me have . . ."[2] And they gave Him a piece of a broiled fish and of an honeycomb. And He took it and did eat before them.'[3]

[1] Jn. 20 : 27.   [2] Lu. 24 : 37-39.   [3] Lu. 24 : 42, 43.

Such a nature was Christ's spiritual body. This was the Body whose hands took solid bread and broke it beside the Emmaus Road.[1] This was the Body whose hands kindled a fire of coals and cooked breakfast of fish and bread for the disciples beside the sea.[2] This was the Body whose feet were held by the worshipping women on Easter Sunday.[3] This was the Body who ' shewed Himself alive after His passion by many infallible proofs, being seen of (His disciples) forty days and speaking of the things pertaining to the Kingdom of God.'[4] Peter insisted that the disciples were those " who did eat and drink with Him after He rose from the dead."[5] And John proclaimed, " That which . . . we have seen with our eyes, which we have looked upon and our hands have handled . . . that which we have seen and heard declare we unto you ! "[6]

We are left in no shadow of a doubt that the spiritual Body of the risen Jesus Christ was of an uncompromisingly physical nature. The witness of the New Testament is here unanimous. It is true that the same Body appears to have passed through closed doors,[7] to have vanished from sight during the Emmaus supper[8] and to have appeared miraculously to Paul as he walked the Damascus road.[9] But these facts cannot undo the undeniably physical nature of the Body with whom the disciples and ' above five hundred brethren '[10] walked and talked and broke bread. They only emphasise the fact that His Body was now endowed with powers which it did not have before. His was a Body which had been raised from the dead by the *Spirit*. It was a spiritual Body. A Spirit-quickened Body. A Spirit-filled Body. This is the Body of which we are members. A Body, let us repeat, which is uncompromisingly physical. A Body which can do greater works than its Lord ever did

[1] Lu. 24 : 30.   [2] Jn. 21 : 9, 13, 15.   [3] Mt. 28 : 9.   [4] Acts 1 : 3.
[5] Acts 10 : 41.   [6] 1 Jn. 1 : 1-3.   [7] Jn. 20 : 19.   [8] Lu. 24 : 31 ; cf. Acts 8 : 39.
[9] Acts 9 : 3.   cf. Acts 18 : 9 ; 23 : 11 ; 27 : 23 ; Ro. 1 : 9.   [10] 1 Cor 15 : 6.

before He rose from the dead.[1] A Body which possesses supernatural powers to accomplish that which would seem impossible to men.

This spiritual Body, we say, was endowed with supernatural powers. And we must go on to say that this element of power is one of the most distinctive characteristics of the ' spiritual ' in the New Testament. Παράκλητος, which is translated ' Comforter' in the King James' version of the Bible, means ' the author or source of strength.'[2] This strength or power is to be seen, not only in the Body of Christ after the resurrection, but also throughout His life—and always in association with the Spirit.

" The Holy Spirit shall come upon thee," said the angel to Mary, " and the *power* of the Highest shall overshadow thee : therefore also that holy thing which shall be born of thee shall be called the Son of God."[3] When Jesus is baptised with the Spirit, He hears a voice from heaven which, as Luke points out,[4] speaks of the Royal Psalm [5] in which God gives *power* and dominion over all the earth to His Son. Jesus is led by the Spirit to be tempted in the wilderness and returns in the *power* of the Spirit into Galilee.[6] His first words in the synagogue at Nazareth are, " The Spirit of the Lord is upon Me . . ."[7] and those in the synagogue are astonished at His *power*.[8]

This close association of the Spirit with power continues with the post-resurrection appearances of Christ. He commands His disciples to wait in Jerusalem until they ' receive *power* after that the Holy Spirit is come ' upon them.[9] Thus it was that, after Pentecost, the spiritual Body

[1] I Jn. 14: 12.   [2] G. S. Hendry, *The Holy Spirit in Christian Theology*, Westminster Press, 1956, p. 50.   [3] Lu. 1: 35.   [4] Acts 13: 33.   [5] Psa. 2, esp. v. 7.   [6] Lu. 4: 14.   [7] Lu. 4: 18.   [8] Lu. 4: 32; cf. Mk. 6: 2.   [9] Acts 1: 8.

of Christ, the Church, went out into the world in ' the *power* of the Holy Ghost.' [1] It's ministry was ' in demonstration of the Spirit and of *power*.' [2] It was bold to preach the Gospel in face of all manner of persecution, for ' God did not give us a spirit of timidity but a Spirit of *power*.' [3] And when the aged Paul looked back over his long ministry, he attributed everything which he had done and said to " what Christ has wrought in me . . . by the *power* of the Holy Spirit." [4]

There was a day in the life of Christ when He was led by the Spirit to a high mountain top. There He was shown all the kingdoms of the world and heard the devil say, " All this power will I give thee . . . if thou . . . wilt worship me."[5] But ' in the power of the Spirit ' [6] He resisted the devil and began His public ministry. There came another day when His ministry was done and He led His disciples up into a high mountain. (Was it, perchance, the same mountain?) And, in the power of the Spirit, He gave them their great commission, " All power is given unto Me in heaven and in earth. Go ye *therefore* and make disciples of all nations . . . and lo, I am with you alway, even unto the end of the world." [7]

Small wonder that, a few weeks later, we find Peter miraculously healing the sick,[8] and raising the dead,[9] and preaching the Gospel with such power that the fruits of his first proclamation were three thousand souls [10] and the fruits of his second were five thousand.[11] Here was a man who knew what the Church *was*, one who understood the essential nature of the Body of Christ. He represented a Church which was deeply conscious of the fact that it was, in very truth, the spiritual Body of Christ in all its physical, powerful, Spirit-filled reality. ' The power of God', he

[1] Ro .15 : 13, A.R.S.V.   [2] 1 Cor. 2 : 4.   [3] 2 Tim. 1 : 7, A.R.S.V.   [4] Ro. 15 : 18f. A.R.S.V.   [5] Lu. 4 : 1-7.   [6] Lu. 4 : 14.   [7] Mat. 28 : 18 f.   [8] Acts 3 : 7, 9 : 34.   [9] Acts 9 : 37 f.   [10] Acts 2 : 41.   [11] Acts 4 : 4.

wrote in later years ' hath given unto us all things that
pertain unto life and godliness,' because it has made us
' partakers in the divine nature.' [1] This was the nature
of the One who had healed the sick and raised the dead
and given His Church all the power in heaven and in earth
—the spiritual Body of Christ.

The Church, we repeat, knew what it was. It was
nothing less than the spiritual Body of Christ. And that
meant that it had its roots, its essence and its destiny in
Jesus Christ Himself. Its nature was the same as the
physical nature of the Christ who had been raised by
the Spirit from the dead. It enjoyed all the powers of that
same Christ. It could and did exercise these powers for His
glory.

Now, if these were the only reasons for using the word
' spiritual ' in relation to the Body of Christ, it would be a
word charged with substantial meaning and dynamic. But
these are not the only reasons. The word has a deeper
significance which carries us to the very heart of the
Gospel and which throws a flood of light upon the nature
of the Church.

It is possible for us to think of the Church as the Body
of Christ and for our thought to remain in the realm of
abstract ideas and impersonal forces. But, if we take
seriously that which is spiritual in a distinctively Christian
sense, we find ourselves entering the realm of that which
is, above all else, intensely *personal*. And it is precisely this
personal content which lifts Christian spirituality right out
of the world of ancient Greece and of Indian mysticism
into the world where the living, historical Jesus Christ is
both the life and the Lord of the Church.

Spiritual blessings and spiritual gifts and spiritual Body

[1] 2 Pet. 1 : 3, 4.

are called ' spiritual ' because they are brought out of the realm of objective reality and into the realm of personal experience and subjective reality by one who is called Holy Spirit. Without the personal activity of God's Spirit, Christ and all His benefits would have little more significance for us than a splendid oil painting of the most inspiring figure in history. He would remain beyond us. An Object of study. Equipped with glorious attributes. But still an Object—an It and not a Thou. He would be like the God of the Moslem whose personality has been burned away in the fire of his austere attributes. He would be like the Buddhist conception of man—nothing more than a bundle of *skandhas* or attributes apart from which there is no person at all. He would be something to be experienced and to be used; something to be taken into account and utilised for the great Cause. But He would not be One with whom we might enter into personal relation. He would remain, as it were, a distant Face . . . out there, beyond.

> *O lonely Face like a star in the night . . .*
> *O fainter echoing footstep !* [1]

And yet, He is the One who meets us, who enters into personal relation with us, who becomes, not a Face, nor an Object, nor an It but a Thou—a familiar Thou. " How can these things be ? "

It is not possible for sinful man to see and know God in Christ as He really is. Natural man can only comprehend those things which are of the earth, earthy—and only that in a broken, fragmentary fashion. And if a Man should approach this natural man, a Man alike in appearance to all other men, wearing the same flesh, subject to the same temptations, living the same life, dying the same death—

[1] Martin Buber. ' *I and Thou.*' tr. R. G. Smith, T. & T. Clark, 1937, p. 42.

is it possible that a man should perceive that *this* Man is
not only Man but God? *God* coming to meet him in all
the fulness of His mercy and His grace. Offering him all
the blessings of heaven and all the blessings of earth as
well! Is it possible? No, it is not possible. Man, little
man, has neither the eyes nor the mind with which to see.
The only eyes which can see Jesus Christ as He really is
are the eyes of God Himself. All the work of Christ is of
no avail for men unless they receive the eyes of the living
God with which to see and to appropriate the Person of
the Son. So it is that God comes to us—God the Spirit—
in all the fulness of His personal presence, entering into
our innermost being so that by Him, in Him and through
Him we see and know the Saviour as *our* Saviour! *Then*
Christ steps out of the world of Object and into the world
of Subject where we meet Him, recognise Him and love
Him face to face as our familiar Friend. This is the work
of the Holy Spirit.

' God sent forth His Son . . . so that we might receive
adoption as sons.' What gracious condescension! But the
news is only half told! For ' God has sent the Spirit
of His Son into our *hearts*, crying. " Abba, Father! " [1]
In that dramatic moment at Cæsarea Philippi when the
first man cried, " Thou art the Christ, the Son of the living
God! ", the answering cry came back to knock all the
props of human pride away—" Flesh and blood have not
revealed it unto thee, but My Father which is in heaven."
This was the work of the Spirit of truth sent by Jesus from
the Father.[2] " I will send (Him) unto you, . . . even the Spirit
of truth . . . He shall testify of Me." [3] Without the Spirit
we are bound in the world of It. We may walk with Christ
for three long years, witnessing His marvellous works,
hearing His gracious words, touching not only the

[1] Gal. 4: 4-6 A.R.S.V.; cf. Ro. 8: 15.   [2] Jn. 14: 16.   [3] Jn. 15: 26; 16: 13, 14.

hem of His garment but handling His Body as well.[1] But unless the Spirit opens our hearts and our eyes we remain as blind and as captive as Judas . . . bound down in the realm of It.

The Spirit is the Spirit who sets us free.[2] Free, that is, to receive the Person of Jesus Christ into our very being. Free to echo the cry of the Son in the Garden of Gethsemane, " Abba, Father ! "—for *we* have become sons ! And, when the Spirit gives us this freedom, we enter the company of those who, ' with unveiled face, beholding the glory of the Lord, are being changed into His likeness from one degree of glory to another. For," Paul hastens to add, " this comes from the Lord who is the Spirit." [3]

It is at this crucial point, when the Church cries, " Abba, Father ! " that we see the supreme significance of the title —the ' Spiritual Body of Christ.' God, for us, is Person. That which is ' spiritual ' has its source, its content and its goal in a *Person*. That which is ' spiritual ' implies not only ' all power in heaven and in earth,' it implies power as it comes to us in a *Person*. He who once belonged to the world of objects, of things, of Its has become Person . . . for *us*. And He has made us person, too. He has made us partakers in *His* life, in His real, flesh and blood, personal, Spirit-filled life. When God formed man of the dust of the earth, He did not leave him as a lifeless thing of clay. He breathed, He inspired His Spirit into him 'and man became a living soul.' [4] When Jesus Christ was risen from the dead, He did not leave His disciples to make their way in the world in their own poor strength. He breathed on them and said, " Receive the Holy Ghost." [5] They became the spiritual Body of Christ.

The Church is not the Body of Christ in any impersonal

---

[1] cf. " This is My Body broken for you."   [2] 2 Cor. 3 : 17.   [3] 2 Cor. 3 : 18. A.R.S.V.   [4] Gen. 2 : 7 ; cf. Ezek. 37 : 1-14.   [5] Jn. 20 : 22 A.R.S.V.

sense. She is not partaker in the divine nature in a sub-personal fashion. The sacred frontiers of personality are not here broken down and done away so that we enter into some mystical realm in which we are ' drenched in divinity ' in such a manner as to de-personalise both God and man. We do not un-God God. And God does not un-man man. Rather does He affirm man in all the splendour of his new-found and fully human personality. For the Spirit who gives this title to the Body of Christ is the personal Spirit of the personal Son. It is He, Jesus Christ, as Person, in whom we persons are partakers. His Body which rose in glory from the dead, His Body which walks the earth to-day as His Church, is no denial of personality. Rather is it a glorious affirmation of the new and truly human personality which Christ has ushered into the world.

This, then, is the Church; the New Humanity; the Spiritual Body of Christ. She is partaker in His divine-human nature, in His power, in His very Person. Yet— let us repeat—this Church, so full of power and grace, so unconditionally partaker in the life of God Himself, is not abroad in the world under her own authority. This Spiritual Body has a Head. It has a Sovereign Lord. And this vital truth is also enshrined in the title, the ' Spiritual Body.' For, whilst the task of the Spirit is so to minister Christ to the Church as to make her partaker in His nature, the second great office of the Spirit is ever to bring the Church under the Lordship of Christ.

The Spirit bears witness not to Himself but to the Person of Jesus Christ, " He shall testify of *Me*.[1] He shall not speak of Himself . . . He shall glorify *Me* : for He shall receive of Mine and shall show it unto you." [2] This is the Spirit who gives the Church not only life but also direction.

[1] Jn. 15 : 26.   [2] Jn. 16 : 13 f.

78

He points neither to Himself nor to the Church. He points to Jesus Christ. He brings the Church under the daily judgment of Jesus Christ. He sets the Church's course in history by Jesus Christ. It is because of His powerful work that the living, personal Jesus Christ is both the life and the Lord of His Church.

Part Two

"THEREFORE . . ."

"THEREFORE ..."

THE NEW TESTAMENT conception of the Church as the Body of Christ abroad in the world in living communion with its sovereign Lord is a grand, sublime conception. It is lofty theology.

Yet we are all too familiar with the divorce between our stirring theology and our pedestrian, work-a-day lives. It may be that we know full well the theology of our situation—" But," we protest, " we are faced with urgent, practical problems to which our grand theology has little or nothing to say!" And so we order our lives in the real world by pre-suppositions which do not have their roots in the life and the death and the resurrection of Jesus Christ our Lord.

We believe with all our hearts that the Incarnation, the Cross and the Resurrection *should* determine and direct the whole life of the Church in the world. We know full well that they do not. And hence we are uneasy men.

For we know that until Christ Himself, Crucified and Risen, is the substance and the Sovereign of all that we do, we are living on a purely humanitarian level and not in the realm in which we are meant to live—the realm of miracle, the realm of the impossible, the realm in which we take up the Pauline cry, not only, "I believe!", but—"I believe, *therefore* . . ."

CHAPTER FIVE

SO SEND I YOU

WE ARE left in no doubt concerning the fundamental nature of the Church's mission to mankind, for we have as starting point our knowledge of the eternal will of the Trinity. We know what His will is because we know what His will was. It was the will of God that all men should be made at one with Him. It was His will that this object should be accomplished by means of a divine mission. God sent His Son, and He sent Him in a particular way, a way which the Church must follow if she is to be faithful to a mission which is not her own but which is God's.

God's mission was accomplished by His coming into *the world*, by His humbling Himself, and by His taking upon Himself the form of a servant ; [1] by His so identifying Himself with sinful men as to gather them up into His very being, making them one with Him for ever.

This was no pseudo-spiritual identification. It was thoroughly materialistic. It involved an Incarnation, an uncompromising union of God with the flesh of sinful men.

This divine mission was foreshadowed in the Old Covenant which was no abstract, disembodied Covenant but was cut into the very flesh of Israel by the rite of circumcision. It was established by the Word of God spoken on Sinai and by the visible exodus from Egypt. It was interpreted by the Decalogue and by the physical

[1] Phil. 2 : 6 ff.

liturgy in the temple. It was continued by the prophetic Word and by the sacrifice of beasts. It was fulfilled and surpassed when the eternal Word became flesh, when God the Son identified Himself with all men in order that all men might be saved.

We have already sought to show how this was accomplished not only upon the Cross but throughout the life of Jesus. His whole life was a self-emptying, a humbling, a giving of Himself to men. His whole life was the outworking of the divine mission; a mission which was certainly not without joy but which plumbed such depths of suffering as pass our understanding.

This was *God's* way of mission.

And, with this background, we look beyond the Cross to the scene in the upper room. The disciples are standing in the presence of their Lord awaiting His command. How were they to conduct themselves in the world? How was Christ's mission to be continued in them? Jesus expressed the nature of their mission in one luminous sentence—" As my Father hath sent Me, even so send I you." [1] *He* had been sent to identify Himself unreservedly with men, to share their sorrows, their griefs, their sufferings; to penetrate into the depths of their lives, to be wounded, to bleed and to die. That was how the Father had sent Him. And now—" So send I you ! "

Christ had known for a long time—probably since His baptism,[2] and certainly since Cæsarea Philippi [3]—that His mission involved death for Himself. But He had also known that it would involve death for those who followed Him. He had repeatedly warned them of the fact.

On the first occasion that He spoke of the Church, He spoke of the *sufferings* of the Church—" If any man will come after Me, let him deny himself and take up his cross

[1] Jn. 20 : 21.   [2] Mk. 1 : 11 ; cf. Isa. 42 : 1-4.   [3] Mat. 16 : 21.

and follow me." [1] He had warned His disciples that the servant was not greater than his Lord,[2] that if men had persecuted Him they would certainly persecute them.[3] "Then shall they deliver you up to be afflicted," He had told them, " and (they) shall kill you." [4] And, as He went up to Jerusalem to the death which He was to accomplish there,[5] He warned them again, " Ye shall . . . drink of the cup that I drink of; and with the baptism that I am baptised withal shall ye be baptised." [6]

We may be sure that if there had been any other way of fulfilling His mission, He would certainly have chosen it. He did not want to suffer and to die. " If it be possible, let this cup pass from Me ! " But it was *not* possible. There was no other way. And the fact that, despite the agony it caused Him, He deliberately chose this way ('He stedfastly set His face to go to Jerusalem.' [7]) knowing that He was choosing it for Himself and for His disciples—this is a fact which drives us to the inescapable conclusion that this was the only way in which God's mission could be fulfilled. The Father was willing to sacrifice His Beloved—" It *pleased* the Lord to bruise Him." [8] Now the Son is willing to sacrifice His beloved [9]—" So send I you." We can only conclude that there is no other way for the Church to accomplish her mission save the way which Christ Himself pursued—the way of the Cross, the way of suffering, the way of the Incarnation.

Now the kind of incarnation which God desires is expressed in the one word ' Immanuel '—God with us.[10] It is an incarnation which demands that we shall really be *with* men; not that we shall speculate or theorise *about* men, but that we shall be *with* men. Like Ezekiel, son of

[1] Mat. 16: 24.   [2] Jn.13: 16.   [3] Jn. 15: 20.   [4] Mat. 24: 9.   [5] Lu. 9: 31.   [6] Mk. 10: 39; cf. Jn. 17: 18.   [7] Lu. 9: 51.   [8] Isa. 53: 10.   [9] cf. Mk. 10: 30—' with persecutions.'   [10] Mt. 1: 23.

man, to sit with men in their shame.[1] To let their sorrows
become our sorrows, to shoulder their burdens, to rot with
them, to die with them. And thus to follow Him whom
God made to be *sin* for us,[2] to fill up that which is lacking
in His sufferings.[3]

The Church is defined, in one of the memoranda drawn
up in preparation for the Augsburg Confession,[4] as the
community of those ' who are persecuted and martyred for
the Gospel's sake.' To be a member of this Church is to
be a witness. To be a witness (μάρτυς) is to be a martyr.
And to be martyred is normal Christian living.

Over against the world, the Christian has no rights of
any kind. He is the servant of all men, for he is the servant
of the Crucified. And the servant is *not* greater than his
Lord. His Lord was led like a sheep to the slaughter and
now He addresses His servant as His ' sheep,' for His
servant is to stand in the place of the Lamb of God who
sacrificed His life for many.[5] The servant—as a member
of Christ's body, the Church—is to be sacrificed. He is to
be lain upon the altar. He is to be taken, like the eucharistic
bread, in the hands of His Lord ; he is to be taken and
blessed and *broken* . . . and given for the sins of the world.[6]
He is to be crucified . . .

Now this crucifixon is not an end in itself. The object
of crucifixion is resurrection. The way in which the
resurrection life of Jesus Christ was let loose in the world
was the way of the Cross. And it is ever thus. If there is
one great theme which runs through the pages of the New
Testament it is this—*No Cross : no Resurrection*. If there
is to be a resurrection in the life of Christ, in the life of the

---

[1] Ez. 3 : 15 ; cf. 9 : 4, in which the men who weep for their brethren are
those with the sign of a cross on their forehead.   [2] 2 Cor. 5 : 21.   [3] Col.
1 : 24.   [4] Quoted by D. Bonhoeffer, *Cost of Discipleship*, S.C.M., 1951, p. 74.
[5] Ro. 8 : 36 ; 9 : 3 ; Phil. 2 : 7, A.R.S.V. ; 1 Thes. 2 : 8.   [6] Mk. 14 : 22.

Church, in the life of the believer, there must first be a crucifixion.

To the world, such an affirmation is utterly absurd. And that for an excellent reason. The world does not believe in resurrection. Why should it believe in crucifixion? For the Church, such a statement presents a problem only when she forgets that she is the real Body of Christ pursuing the same goal as her Lord pursued, and pursuing it *by the same means*. At the entrance to the Church there is a font where men may be baptised. And baptism is always baptism unto *death*. 'Buried in the waters of baptism.' But the Church in the wilderness [1] emerged from these waters as a new people, who had been given a new world in which to live. Likewise the believer rises from these waters of burial [2] as a new creation, as a member of a new people whose sign is an empty cross. The life of this people is sustained by bread and wine, by Body and by Blood. In the Bible, blood is always the symbol of life and the broken body is the symbol of death. The Church may not have the wine without the bread; she may not have the blood without the flesh; she may not have the life without the death. No Cross: no Resurrection.

That is to say that we do, in fact, possess the unsearchable riches of Christ; [3] we are in fact partakers in the things which God has prepared for those who love Him; [4] we are, in fact, risen with Christ—but this is only *manifest* as we are crucified with Christ. 'Always bearing about in the Body the dying of the Lord Jesus, *that* the life also of Jesus might be made manifest in our body.' [5] In other words, there is but one reason for our crucifixion—' We . . . are alway delivered unto death for Jesus' sake, *that* the

---

[1] Acts 7: 38; Jos. 3: 17.   [2] Ro. 6: 4, 5.   [3] Eph. 3: 8.   [4] I Cor. 2: 9.
[5] 2 Cor. 4: 10.

life also of Jesus might be made manifest in our mortal flesh.'[1] It is the mission of the Church to make manifest the life of Jesus. His life is made manifest in death.[2]

Hence, there *is* a lever by which the Church and the world may be raised into the realm of resurrection. It is a cruciform lever. It is to be found in the lowest place— in a stable, amongst publicans and sinners, on a gibbet between two thieves. It is to be found where God made Himself of no reputation, where He humbled Himself and experienced what the world called abject failure. Now His follower is one who ' fails ' as well, for he sees his failure ' as a kind of condition of the final victory. He adds his own failure to the great stream that is sweeping on to ultimate triumph.'[3]

This is the movement of mission because it is the movement of the Incarnation. It is a downward movement which leads men up to God. If we are to ascend with Christ we must first *descend* with Him into the lowest parts of the earth.[4] If we would reign with Christ, we must first die with Christ.[5]

Now the missionary significance of our death with Christ is that the world begins to believe. Men believe for the same reason that they believed two thousand years ago. They believe because they know that they are face to face with God—with God Himself, in Christ Crucified. And until Christ Crucified takes on visible form the world will not believe. " Except I shall see in His hands the print of the nails, and put my finger into the print of the

---

[1] 2 Cor. 4: 11.   [2] It was not until Christ had actually died that the veil of the temple was rent in twain and a way was made for all mankind into the Holy of Holies. Not until that moment do we hear the first Gentile confession of faith, " Truly this man was the Son of God ! " Mk. 15 : 39. [3] Abbé Michonneau, *The Missionary Spirit in Parish Life*, Mercier Press, Cork, 1952, p. 86.   [4] Eph. 4: 9, 10.   [5] 2 Tim. 2: 11 f; cf. Gen. 32: 24 ff.; Rev. 7: 14-17; 5: 10; 22: 5.

nails . . . I will not believe ! " [1] This is precisely what the
world says to the Church. We who talk of walking the
way of the Cross dare not show men our hands. For we
have not been wounded for them, we have not suffered
for them. We have done little more than *preach* for them.
And we cannot convince the world by our preaching of
the Cross when we shrink from the Cross in our own lives.
But when the world *sees* as well as hears—when the world
sees, as it were, the print of the nails in our hands, *then*
the world will have seen not only us but our Lord. And
men will echo Thomas's confession of faith—" My Lord
and my God ! " [2]

And yet the world will not only believe. There are
those in the world who will be too afraid to believe. They
will fear the power of that Church which has forsaken all
to follow Christ. Like its Lord, such a Church has an
immense strength. It has abandoned literally everything
but Christ. There is no hold which the world can get
upon it, for it has forsaken the ways of the world and has
embraced the sufferings of God. If men should take its
coat, it will give them its cloak also, though the wind be
keen and cold. This Church travels light. It is poor. It
offers men little more than itself, its very being. This
Church is an intolerable Church which, as Bonhoeffer
insists, is ' bound to provoke the world to insult, violence
and slander. Too menacing, too loud are the voices of these
poor meek men, too patient and too silent their suffering.
Too powerful are the testimony of their poverty and their
endurance of the wrongs which the world inflicts on them.
This is intolerable, and so, while Jesus calls them blessed,
the world cries : " Away with them, away with them ! " [3]

But whether men cry " Away with them ! " or whether
they cry " My Lord and my God ! "—at least they *cry*.

[1] Jn. 20 : 25 ; cf. 10 : 37 f.   [2] Jn. 20 : 28.   [3] *Cost of Discipleship*, p. 97 f.

They are no longer indifferent. They do not ignore the Church, as they did not ignore the Christ. They do not conceive the Church to be utterly irrelevant. The Church has become not 'Words, words, words,' but a live, compelling question-mark which demands an answer.

" *Why* do these men come down and dwell amongst us ?
  Why do they give us of their substance and their life ?
  Why do they share our sorrows and our burdens ?
  Why do they bind up our wounds with such compassion ?
  Why do they weep when we are weeping ?
  Why do they mourn when we are mourning ?
  Do they want to be crucified ?
  Like Christ ? "

When the world begins to ask such questions, the Church may begin to lift up her head. For her redemption, and the redemption of the world, draweth nigh.

There are, to-day, not a few voices which insist that the missionary Church must identify herself in uncompromising fashion with the world to which she is sent. She must do so, it is said, in as radical a manner as her Lord identified Himself with men.

But this word 'identification' is often misunderstood and misused. We do not doubt that Christ identified Himself with men. 'The Word *was* made flesh.' God 'made Him to be *sin* for us.'[1] And this was a creative identification because He was also 'without sin.'[2] We who are of the Church are not without sin. And hence we are urged to be conformed to the 'image of God'[3] or to the 'image of Christ,'[4] but we are never urged to be

[1] 2 Cor. 5 : 21 ; cf. Ro. 8 : 3.   [2] Heb. 4 : 15.   [3] 1 Cor. 11 : 7; Col. 3 : 10.
[4] Ro. 8 : 29; 2 Cor. 3 : 18.

conformed to the image of the world. Rather do we hear the cry—" Be *not* conformed to this world, but be ye *transformed* . . ." [1] If we seek to identify ourselves, *in the first place*, with the world, there can be no doubt that our mission will fail. For there is a serious sense in which we need make no effort to be conformed to and identified with the world. We are already so identified in a negative manner. The world is a sinful world. And we are sinners. *Jesus* identified Himself with the world. But we stand on different ground from Jesus. He humbled Himself. We can't. There is no lower place for us to go. Simply to seek a more visible identification of ourselves with men is vain. And, in any case, it is pointless. There is no profit in *our* identifying ourselves with men. Men do not need *us*. They need *Christ*.

That is why the primary need of the missionary Church is not to identify herself with the world but to identify herself with her Lord.

There is a great gulf between God and the world and it cannot be crossed by men. It is a gulf which yawns between Christian and non-Christian, and *neither* of them can bridge it. It can only be bridged by the One who has already bridged it, the Mediator between God and men. And if the Church would continue the mission of her Lord, she can only do so by becoming so identified with Him that His life becomes her life, and His Cross (which spans the gulf) becomes her Cross as well. She must begin with God-in-Christ and not with man.

Unless she begins with God-in-Christ, man's basic sin appears in her. It is the desire to be like God—" And ye shall be as gods." [2] But it is the distinctive characteristic of Christianity [3] to have God rather than man as start

---

[1] Ro. 12 : 2.   [2] Gen. 3 : 5.   [3] And of her forebear, Judaism.

point, to be theocentric and not anthropocentric. To abandon this fundamental position is to abandon the Church's source of life; it is to abandon all hope of doing anything more than *modify* the world which she is commissioned to convert.

But, beginning with God, beginning with Christ, beginning with an identification of her life with His—then all things are possible.

Yet it must be a *total* identification in which the Church denies herself completely. It must be an identification in which she cuts herself off once and for all from that which is merely "I" and unites herself, in the most literal and uncompromising way, with Jesus Christ her Lord. And is this impossible? Is it beyond man's power? It is certainly beyond man's power but it is not impossible. It has been *done*. But not by man. It has been done by Christ. It has been done in His life, His death, His resurrection. It is an accomplished *fact*. This is the Gospel! Not that *we* will unite ourselves with God but that *God* has united Himself with us. "It is finished!" All that remains is that the Church should believe. And that, believing, she should become what God has made her. And that, becoming, she should go out into the world bearing Christ's life to men.

This believing, this becoming, this going forth will involve an act of the will, a radical break with the standards of the world, a break that will, no doubt, leave an angry wound. But the Church may not complain that this break is unreasonable. The Cross of Christ is not reasonable. Sin is not reasonable, and that is what sent Him to the Cross. Love is not reasonable, and that is what compelled Him to go there. The way of identification with the Crucified is no reasonable way. But it is the only way by which the Church can bring the life of God to the world.

In the second place, so far as the individual Christian is concerned, identification must involve identification with the Church. Christ gave Himself *especially* to the Church.[1] Likewise, the believer, after giving himself to Christ, must give himself *especially* to the Church. The gifts of God are not given to the believer as an individual; they are given to the household of faith. The Church alone receives the sacrament of Christ's Body and Blood, His death and life. The believer is but one member of the Body; if he would draw upon the resources of the whole organism, he must be deeply grafted into the Church. It was weakness at this point which, in large measure, accounted for the partial failure of the French priest-workers, many of whom went for months with no flesh and blood encounter with the Church, either in the Sacrament or in face to face meeting with other priests. And, hence, they found it increasingly difficult to distinguish between that which was of the Gospel and that which was of the world. They needed the Church. And they needed it in tangible, corporeal form.

No doubt the Christian derives his life from Jesus Christ alone. But Christ comes to him in an especially powerful way through his brother. It is from his brother that the Christian must receive the bread and the wine. It is from his brother's lips that he must hear the Word of God. That Word will sometimes be a Word of judgment. In the absence of his brother, the isolated believer may, for example, conjure up his dream of mission. He may love his *dream* of the Church's mission more than he loves the Church's *mission*. He may insist that his dream be realised

[1] 1 Tim. 4: 10.

94

by God. His dream must be shattered. It must be shattered by the Body of which he is but a single member. It must be shattered by his brother who, if he loves him, will speak God's Word of re-creative judgment. And it is from the same brother that he must hear God's Word of mercy —the word of pardon; the word which lightens his darkness and warms his heart, which brings encouragement and hope and vision; the word which makes him a new creation time and again.

The disciples' dependence on their membership in the Body was very clearly recognised in the apostolic age. The first Christians did not only continue ' stedfastly in the apostles' doctrine and . . . in breaking of bread and in prayers '—they also continued stedfastly in ' fellowship.' [1] It was this fellowship—or, rather, Christ in this fellowship —which gave power and substance to the doctrine, the sacrament and the prayers. It is, no doubt, for this reason that, in every instance [2] of missionary endeavour recorded in the book of Acts, there are at least two disciples involved. For the same reason, also, Jesus sent out His disciples, not singly, but ' by two and two.' [3]

The Christian *believes* in the communion of saints. For the communion of saints is the Body of Christ. The Christian *needs* the saints. He needs them because he needs Christ.

But the supreme importance of the identification of the Christian with the Church is its importance for the world. The agent of mission is not, in the first place, the individual Christian. The agent of mission is the Church. It is the community which converts. The mission of the Church is to proclaim Christ by her community life. It is not only to verbalise Christ's forgiveness. It is to *live* as the com-

[1] Acts 2 : 42.   [2] With the single exception of Philip, Acts 8 : 26 ff.   [3] Mk. 6 : 7; Lu. 10 : 1.

munity of forgiven and forgiving sinners. It is not only to assert that Christ brings His life to men. It is to live His life in such a way that Christ is ' placarded ' before men's eyes. *Tell* men that they can be partakers in God's nature and they may be mildly interested or, perchance, mildly amused. Confront them with a community which reflects the life of God in Christ and that is quite a different matter. A community, that is to say, in which participation in the nature of God is the bed-rock foundation of the whole of its life and work. Such a community can only be described as a colony of heaven, quite unlike anything else in the world. It is a living demonstration of the Kingdom that is to come, the Kingdom that is at hand, that is in the midst. It convinces the world of sin because the world sees holiness.[1] It sees it in the communion of saints, the Body of Christ on earth.

For the sake of the Christian, for the sake of the Church, and for the sake of the world, the member must be identified with the Body.

And yet all this is quite without avail for the missionary purpose of God unless the Christian and the Church become identified with *the world*. " As Thou hast sent Me into the world, even so have I also sent them into the world." [2] This, as we have seen, is a ' sending ' by way of incarnation, of suffering, of crucifixion. We have seen that there is no other way for the Church. No Cross : no Resurrection. This is the way in which the Church begins to *understand* the world. It is also the way which holds out a possibility that the Church will begin to be *understood* by the world. It is the only way of mission through which the Church wins the right to be heard. For it is no hit and

[1] cf. Max Warren, *The Truth of Vision*, Canterbury Press, 1948, p. 138. [2] Jn. 17 : 18.

run mission. It is no brief encounter. It is a life-long engagement. It is an engagement on the part of those who have been so united with Jesus Christ that no man is able to touch them except he touch Christ also. It is an engagement on the part of those whose lives are so interpenetrated with the life of Christ that their sufferings are truly His sufferings, and hence they are creative sufferings, redemptive, divine. It is an engagement in which the Christian goes out into the world as a debtor to all men, as public property, as a man with no rights except the right of bearing his cross. He goes out as his Lord went out, to be sacrificed for the sins of the world. He goes out, as Abbé Michonneau affirms,[1] as a *victim*. His rightful place is on the altar where the unbelieving multitudes pass by. ' Without shedding of blood there is no remission of sins.' His blood must be shed. For the blood of the martyrs must be mingled with the blood of the Lord if it is to become the seed of the Church.

What, in concrete terms, does this involve? When Kagawa lived in the Tokyo slums, he embraced precisely the same conditions as those to whom he was sent—he never killed less than forty-five bedbugs in a night.[2] When Father Loew engaged in mission to the dock workers of Marseilles, he found himself dining off the contents of a garbage pail.[3] But the external manifestations of a serious attempt to break down the wall which separates the Church from the world will, of course, vary according to the circumstances of the particular mission field involved. It will affect the site and the size of the minister's or missionary's home; it will affect his income, his manner of dress, his whole style of life. It will involve many lesser external factors which, precisely because they are ' lesser ' factors,

[1] *op. cit.*, p. 83.　　[2] *Love the Law of Life*, S.C.M., 1934, p. 184.　　[3] *Mission to the Poorest*, Sheed & Ward, 1950, p. 42.

will be much more difficult to renounce or to accept in the absence of the plaudits of observers.[1]

But, if nothing more than these external factors is involved, there is no real identification. For these factors, like the sacraments, should be an outward and a visible sign of an inward and an invisible reality—a sign of that complete self-emptying, that self-denial, that unreasonable acceptance of the world which was made manifest in Christ. There is an interior acceptance, an interior identification, which revolutionises the fundamental attitudes of the Christian and which brings forth the fruit of a deep and sympathetic unity with the world. The rooting out of class, or national, pride ; the thoroughgoing recognition that one is a sinner like the men to whom one goes ; the entering into their tragedies and griefs so that one actually bears their burdens—these are amongst the internal factors which issue in an at-one-ment. They all involve suffering. They are all terribly costly. They are all indispensable conditions for those engaged in the mission of Christ.

Now it would be idle to pretend that this movement of mission, of deep identification, is anything other than a movement from which we naturally shrink. It is the movement of ' love in practice ' which, in Dostoievsky's words, ' is a harsh and terrible thing compared with love in dreams.' It is easy to speak or to write about this love, and to do so with passionate conviction. But such a passion may well be a substitute for a Passion of a higher order. We know that God does not want our passions, our emotions, so much as He wants our lives. In the realm of mission, He does not want an incarnational theology.

[1] cf. S. Kierkegaard, *Gospel of Sufferings*, tr. Aldworth and Ferrie, James Clarke, 1955, p. 18.

He wants an incarnation. 'The Cross as dogma,' writes Thomas Kelly, 'is painless speculation. The Cross as lived suffering is anguish and glory.'[1] And when the nails bite deep one is more conscious of the anguish than the glory.

There is, perhaps, a certain romance in the theology of identification. There is romance in the very blackness of Good Friday when the crowds look on at the dramatic scene, if not with admiration, then at least with interest. There is certainly romance in the glory of Easter Sunday when the stone has been rolled away and " Christ is risen indeed ! " But the identification with which we are concerned speaks little of the Friday and the Sunday. For the most part it speaks of the unnamed Saturday between. All the crowds have gone away ; they are back in their homes ; they have forgotten. This is the day of burial. It is the day that most men live. That is why it is the day of *identification*—of serious, sober, unadorned identification.

He who has caught a glimpse of the nature of this way of mission will certainly not wish to follow it. If he *seeks* crucifixion, he may be sure that he does not know what he is seeking. He is seeking God-forsakenness. "Why hast Thou forsaken Me ? " He who knows the true nature of this crucifixion cries, " Father, *save Me* from this hour ! " But if, whilst understanding what he does, he is able to go on to say, " Nevertheless, not my will but Thine be done," we may be sure that the holy will of God will indeed be done and that it will be identical with that will which Christ followed all the days of His life. It will lead to joy in heaven and on earth, no doubt. But it will lead there by way of Calvary.

But once the Church steps out upon this way, not

[1] *A Testament of Devotion*, Friends Home Service Committee, 1949, p. 57.

knowing whither she goes, and realising that she has no right to know whither she goes ; once she strikes her tents and steps out into the wilderness of the world, she discovers that which she could never have discovered inside her settled camp. She discovers that her Lord is to be found *outside* the camp ; that His real presence is most perfectly known when she is involved in this world for which He died, when she herself is ' without the camp, bearing His reproach.' [1] It was in the midst of thick cloud and fire and earthquake that Moses met with God.[2] It was in the midst of the burning fiery furnace that the servants of the Most High ' walked with the Son of God.' [3] It was to those who were going forth on a mission which involved crucifixion [4] that Christ gave His promise—" I am with you alway." [5] It is on this kind of mission that His promise is proved to be true.

And it is upon this obscure way, this way of the Cross, that the Church finds a holy confidence. She knows that her road leads not only to the Cross but on to the Resurrection. And this knowledge makes her triumph in obscurity. It arms her strongly against desire for success. It makes her *willing* to be rejected, willing to have the Isaac slain in her soul [6] because she has God's promise that a cosmic resurrection is assured.[7] She is well aware that, in this battle, victory goes to those who lose. Not to those who lose the battle—for they are sure of winning it—but to those who lose themselves. She knows that ' victory belongs to those who are willing to lay down their lives in the struggle without asking to see the victory.' [8] For they have *seen* the victory. They have seen it in the face of Jesus Christ.

And this way gives the Church a divine authority which

[1] Heb. 13 : 13.   [2] Ex. 19 : 16 ff.   [3] Dan. 3 : 25.   [4] cf. Jn. 21 : 18 ;
1 Cor. 4 : 11-13 ; 1 Pet. 4 : 12 f., etc.   [5] Mat 28 : 20.   [6] Gen. 22 : 10.
[7] Heb. 11 : 17 ff.   [8] Michonneau, *op. cit.*, p. 84.

is not to be found in the world. Hers is the way of self-forgetful love and she continues on that way though men attack her and deride her. In *this* sense, she knows where she is going. She is going the way of the love of Christ—and that is all that matters. Against His love there are no weapons and there is no law. Men are faced with but two alternatives. They worship or they crucify. Either way God triumphs and the world is brought nearer Easter Sunday.

This way also is the way of holiness. There are many who protest, " If I go this way of identification I am bound to be conformed to the world. The choice is clear. Either I am holy or else I am identified with the world." The truth is that the Christian cannot be holy *unless* he be identified with the world. Neither can he be identified with the world unless he be holy (that is, unless he be identified with the Mediator). ' You are a missionary to the extent you are a saint,' writes Michonneau.[1] ' The struggle for perfection and the missionary effort are . . . so intimately intertwined that they are but one thing.'[2] ' Our sanctification is a necessity for this work,' affirm the Little Sisters of Jesus, who work in a downtown Paris factory, ' and . . . the work itself is sanctifying.'[3] We must see in our corner of the vineyard, says Michonneau again, ' the people who are destined to make saints of us while we are trying to lead them back to God.'[4] The Old Testament priest did not only bear upon his shoulders and his heart the names of the men for whose salvation he laboured.[5] He also bore upon his forehead a golden plate with the words written— ' Holiness to the Lord.'[6] He was holy and he was identified. That was what it meant to be a priest. And if the great High Priest of the Church was made perfect through

[1] *op. cit.*, p. 107.   [2] *ibid.*, p. 108.   [3] Maisie Ward, *France Pagan*, Sheed & Ward, 1950, p. 207.   [4] *Revolution in a City Parish*, Blackfriars, 1951, p. 158. [5] Ex. 28: 12, 29.   [6] Ex. 28: 36.

suffering,[1] will those who follow in His way be made perfect by any other means?

But, most important of all, and as we have already asserted, this way of identification with the world is the way by which the world believes. It believes because it has been confronted by redeemed men and women. "These Christians must show me that they are redeemed before I will believe in their Redeemer!" cried Nietzsche. The Church shows that she has been redeemed—more, she shows forth her Redeemer—when she walks the road which Christ has walked before her. "No man cometh unto the Father, but by Me."[2] Christ went to the Father by way of Calvary. The Church goes to the Father when she walks the same rough way. The world *cannot* go to the Father except it sees that way revealed in terms of flesh and blood. This was God's way of revelation. The Word did not become spirit. The Word became flesh.

[1] Heb. 2: 10.　　[2] Jn. 14: 6; cf. Mat. 11: 27.

CHAPTER SIX

THAT THEY MAY HAVE LIFE

WE TURN now to consider the nature of the Gospel. It is the Gospel of *Christ*—of Incarnation, Crucifixion, Resurrection. And, if it be a Gospel of Incarnation, it will take physical form in a needy, physical world. ' Christianity, wrote Archbishop Temple, is the most avowedly materialist of all the great religions.'[1] It finds expression in healing, in politics, in preaching, in agriculture, in economics, in art. God's concern for the world has never been a purely ' religious ' concern. It has always been a ' worldly ' concern. He *made* the world. He pronounced it " Very good." He bade men have dominion over *the earth*.[2] He promised an *historical* redemption.[3] He enacted social legislation and political laws. In Paul Lehmann's phrase, ' God is a politician ! ' Most of the Biblical images are political images. God is the God of a people and of a covenant. He leads His people out of material bondage, He gives them a land and a government, He sends them into exile, He delivers them, He establishes a Kingdom. He is concerned with peace and war, with foreign policy. For Israel, He is first and foremost ' the Lord thy God which brought thee forth out of the land of Egypt, from the house of bondage.' [4] His prophets insist that observance of religious law is worthless if the economic law is

[1] *Nature, Man and God*, p. 478.　[2] Gen. 1 : 28.　[3] e.g. Isa. 60 : 1-22; 65 : 25; Zech. 14 : 9; Mal. 1 : 11; Hab. 2 : 14; Amos 9 : 11-15.　[4] Deu. 6 : 12; 5 : 6.

neglected—' (Israel has) afflicted the just, they take a bribe and they turn aside the poor . . . therefore the Lord, the God of hosts, the Lord, saith thus ; . . . " I hate, I despise your feast days . . . though ye offer Me burnt offerings . . . I will not accept them." ' [1] " Is not *this* the fast that I have chosen ? To loose the bands of wickedness, to undo the heavy burdens and to let the oppressed go free? Is it not to deal thy bread to the hungry, and that thou bring the poor that are cast out to thy house ? " [2] God gave Israel a Year of Jubilee. It was a year of solemn worship and of praise. But it was also a year when slaves were freed, when debts were cancelled, and when land was returned to the poor.[3] God's law for Israel reflected His nature. It was concerned with government, with property, with hygiene, with agriculture, sacrifice and worship. It was a law from heaven, heavenly. And it was of the earth, earthy.

The ten sacred words of this law were kept in the holy place of the temple, hidden behind the veil. In that supreme Event [4] when the Word Himself took human flesh and bore that flesh through death to life, the veil of the holy place was rent in twain,[5] the Word was let loose in the world and the material was sanctified for ever. By God's irreversible deed, heaven and earth were united in the Body of the Son. By this deed God announced in unmistakable terms the holiness of all things physical. He was so concerned with the things of this world that He took flesh and blood on earth and carried His humanity through death to highest heaven. The Christ who sits at God's right hand to-day is the Christ whose Body rose from the dead and whose Body ascended into heaven. There His new humanity reigns, proclaiming all flesh sacred ; proclaiming God's profound concern for babies born in squalor ; [6] for

---

[1] Amos 5 : 12, 16, 21, 22. [2] Isa. 58 : 6 f. [3] Lev. 25 : 10 ff. [4] דָּבָר means not only ' word ' but also ' thing ' or ' event.' [5] Mat. 27 : 51. [6] Lu. 2 : 7.

refugees who, like Mary, Joseph and Jesus, have fled from homes in fear;[1] for those who are hungry as Christ was their hungry ;[2] for those who are naked as He was naked ;[3] for powerless minorities ;[4] and for all who suffer injustice at the hands of the tyrants of this world.[5]

Now the reason behind God's concern for the material world is to be found in the nature of His love for men. He loves *men*. He does not love abstract, ideal Man, the man who exists only in the head of the philosopher. He loves men as they really are, in all their complex, confused relationships with other men, with nature, with themselves. Loving men as they are, He is concerned for their physical well-being. It matters to God that one man in four has a serious, painful disease of the eye,[6] that two men in three go hungry all their days,[7] and that mental illness occurs in every fourth family in the West.[8] It matters because He loves *men*—with a total, all-embracing love.

All this is manifested in Christ's works of mercy which crowd the pages of the Gospels. On this we need not dwell. We must, however, underline the fact that these works were done without ulterior motive. Christ healed men's bodies, not in order to convert them,[9] but for no better reason than that He loved them. He fed men because they were hungry. He opened their eyes because they were blind. We have to twist and torture the Scriptures to find a 'spiritual' reason behind Christ's every deed. He who had made human flesh His own had a mission to human *flesh*. That mission He passed on to His Church ; it is a mission which she 'spiritualises' at her peril. 'God became incarnate,' writes Jacques Ellul, 'it is not for us to undo

---

[1]Mat. 2 : 14. [2]Lu. 4: 2 ; Jn. 19 : 28. [3]Jn. 19 : 23 ; cf. Mat. 25 : 36, 43. [4]Mat. 26 : 56. [5]Lu. 23 : 14-25 ; cf. Jn. 19 : 12. [6]Trachoma. See World Health Organisation *News-letter*, June, 1955, p. 2. [7]*A Strategy for World Health*, W.H.O., p. 2. [8]cf. Sir David Henderson, *A Textbook of Psychiatry*, O.U.P., 1950, 30-32. D. F. Buckle, W.H.O. *Newsletter*, Dec. 1954, p. 2. [9]e.g. Mat. 17: 14-18 ; Mk. 6 : 56 ; 8 : 22-26 ; Lu. 5 : 12 ff. ; Jn. 5 : 13, etc. etc.

His work.'[1] The mission which Christ passed on to His Church was a mission of ' wholeness '; it was foreshadowed in the ministry of John the Baptist when he called on men not only to repent and to be baptised, but also to share their food and clothing with the poor.[2]

The Church *must* call on men to repent and to be baptised. But if the Church does nothing more than that, she denies the mission and the Gospel which is hers. ' Many will say to Me in that day, " Lord, Lord, have we not prophesied in Thy Name ? " . . . and then will I profess unto them, " I never knew you. Depart from Me ! " '[3] ' If a fellow man or woman has no clothes to wear and nothing to eat, and one of you say, " Good luck to you, I hope you'll keep warm and find enough to eat," and yet give them nothing to meet their physical needs, what on earth is the good of that ? '[4] Christ's words to such men is terribly plain—" Depart from Me, ye cursed, into everlasting fire ! "[5]

The Church was not taught to pray, " Thy Kingdom come in heaven " but " Thy Kingdom come *on earth*," and if she limits her life to preaching and liturgy, she cuts the nerve of her Gospel. If the early Christians had done no more than preach they would have been left in peace. But they were those who were turning *the world* upside down.[6] And their social and economic life constituted a threat to Rome itself.[7] Hence, bitter persecution slew their saints and swelled their ranks. They suffered and they triumphed in every sphere of life. To have done no more than preach would have been to check the fury of the pagan world. But it would also have been to deny their Lord.

[1] *The Presence of the Kingdom*, tr. Olive Wyon, Westminster Press, 1951, p. 14.
[2] Lu. 3 : 11.   [3] Mat. 7 : 22.   [4] Ja. 2: 16, Phillip's *Letters to Young Churches*, Bles, 1953.   [5] Mat. 25 : 41.   [6] Acts 17 : 6.   [7] cf. T. Ralph Morton, *Community of Faith*, Association Press, 1954, p. 39.

It would have been to postpone the conversion of an Empire.

Those who ask in our own day, "Is it not enough simply to preach?" betray a lack of real compassion for the sufferings of their fellows. They display an indifference to the actual situation which others have to endure. Theirs is a spirituality which is not of Christ. It is a spirituality which is used and abused by the world. Hitler insisted that the sole task of the Church was to create integrity in men's hearts. Thus, and thus alone, was she to affect the political scene. The Barmen Declaration was the Church's swift reply—'We reject the false doctrine that there are spheres of life in which we belong, not to Jesus Christ but to other masters; realms where we do not need to be justified or sanctified by Him.'[1]

The Church lives the Gospel into the whole life of the world. She goes out as her Lord went out—to meet men's total need with the all-sufficient grace of God. And this 'grace is love in its princely and sovereign form, love to the indifferent and the disloyal, whose one claim is their need.'[2] The Church does not refuse to heal men's bodies unless they give heed to the preaching of the Word. She knows that that Word alone will meet their deepest need, physical and spiritual. But she has a greater need than theirs in mind. It is a need in the heart of God. His need is to see the immediate pain and hurt of His children healed with all possible speed. He is *not* the Unmoved Mover. He *cares*! And His Church cares too. He knows that the day will come when all sorrow and crying will be done away.[3] But, like Jesus at the grave of Lazarus, knowing that a new day is certain, now, in this agonising moment, He weeps, for He *loves* His children. And He not only

[1] *Die Sechs Sätze der Barmer Theologischen Erklärung vom 31 Mai 1934*, II, 3.
[2] H. R. Mackintosh, *The Christian Apprehension of God*, 1934, 212.   [3] Rev. 21 : 4.

weeps. He *works* that their anguish may be healed. And His Church—if it is *His* Church—works too.

Materialistic Christianity is tremendously popular. It wins the approval of the world. This fact alone is sufficient to condemn it in some men's eyes. But we may not dismiss materialistic Christianity because it gains applause from the world. *Christ* gained applause from the world. He fed the hungry and healed the sick and men cried " Hosanna ! " and cast their coats in His path. The fact that they quite misunderstood His mission did not prevent His caring for their bodies. Even the fact that men's hearts were actually hardened to the Gospel in those very places where He had done most of His deeds of mercy [1] did not stop His meeting their physical needs. He *loved* them. He could do nothing less.

Yet the moment when the Church wins the plaudits of the world is the moment when she must beware. Christ did not promise applause. He promised persecution : " Ye shall be hated of all men . . . they (will) persecute you." [2] The Church's temptation may be Christ's temptation in the desert and on the Cross. It may be a temptation to win men with bread,[3] a temptation merely to alter and not to recreate the world, a temptation to gain a cheap allegiance by means of the spectacular.[4]

The Church, in other words, may be tempted to win the world by its high, sacrificial, social righteousness. But if Christianity is no more than social righteousness the Church has no right to win the world. It stands as one religion amongst many. Its faith is not unique. This demand for social righteousness existed in the world long before Jesus was born ; not only in Judaism but also in

[1] Mat. 11 : 20 ff. [2] Mat. 10 : 22, 23. [3] Lu. 4 : 3. [4] Lu. 4 : 9; Mk. 15 : 32.

the ancient religions of the East. If Christianity be basically social teaching it could quite well thrive without Christ.

But the core of Christianity is not to be found in teaching—not even in the teaching of Christ. It is to be found in Christ Himself. The 1928 Jerusalem Conference affirmed—" Christianity is Christ." It is the Christ who certainly seeks to meet the social needs of men ; but it is also the Christ who knows that when these needs have all been met, men will still be like T. S. Eliot's 'hollow men; ' [1] men with a vacuum in their souls who, ' following after bubbles, have become bubbles themselves.' [2] And, without Christ, they will remain bubbles—elegant, sophisticated, cultured bubbles, perchance—but *bubbles* just the same ; bubbles in whom God's supreme purpose has not been fulfilled. For them, Christ *the Lord* is irrelevant. In their lives God Almighty has been thwarted. They have no personal relationship with Him. They have no personal relationship with men. They have not, in fact, become men at all. They stand on yonder side of creation.

God is Person. His supreme creation is personal life. The goal of history is personal relation. As the life of the Trinity is perfect personal relation, so man moves—or does not move—towards that divine fulfilment. Political pro-grammes, economic schemes, social and medical services, do not, *as such*, bring personal relation. They are of immense importance in God's sight. But, in the highest realm of all, they, in themselves, are neutral. Those who participate in such schemes may endure a ' relation ' like the stars in their courses, each playing his part, keeping out of the other's orbit, never entering into relation, never *meeting*. And where there is no meeting there is no life.

---

[1] ' *The Hollow Men,*' 1925.

[2] Jer. 2 : 5, following George Adam Smith's translation. For the application of this theme to nations and empires see a brilliant passage in Gordon Rupp's *Luther's Progress to the Diet of Worms*, S.C.M., 1951, p. 100.

No life, that is to say, as *God* would have it. For God's supreme aim is to bring men into *relation*. And, above all, to bring men into relation with Himself.

It is in such relation, and only in such relation, that men cease to be passive recipients of divine favour and become active *participants* in God's great scheme of things.

This brings us to the heart of the Gospel, to the heart of Christ's Mission for His Church. It brings us to the two deep notes which can be heard throughout the record of God's dealings with men. There are lighter, higher notes of great significance. But beneath these notes there is the unchanging rhythm which expresses God's deepest purpose for mankind.

If we try to discover the dominant note in Jesus' teaching, and if, for the moment, we limit our search to the Synoptic Gospels, we find, at least on a first reading, that His almost overwhelming emphasis appears to be on doing good,[1] on doing the will of God,[2] and, supremely, on *following* Him.[3] The Sermon on the Mount, for example, calls men to godly living and it sums up this call in the charge to do God's will.[4] Both in Christ's teaching and in His actions it becomes quite clear that this ' will of God ' is, above all else, that men should *follow* Him.

Hence, it is not surprising that many sincere men insist that the sum and the substance of the faith is to be found in Christ's plain words, " Follow Me ! " They are convinced that ' orthodox ' Christianity has buried the straightforward teaching of Jesus beneath a mass of complex dogma and is guilty of nothing less than a disastrous betrayal of the Founder of the faith. They point out that

[1] e.g. Mk. 13 : 34-37 ; Mat. 5 : 7-9, 44, 45 ; 25 : 40 ; Lu. 19 : 9, etc.   [2] e.g. Mat. 21 : 29-31.   [3] e.g. Mat. 5 : 11 ; 10 : 22 ; 24 : 13 ; 16 : 25 ; 19 : 21, 28 ; Mk. 8 : 34, 35 ; Lu. 18 : 22 ; 22 : 28 f. ; cf. Mat. 4 : 18, 22 ; 8 : 19, 22 ; 9 : 9.   [4] Mat. 7 : 21-27.

such issues as forgiveness play a very minor role in the Gospel narratives; that in the earliest Gospel Jesus raises the question of forgiveness on only four occasions,[1] that in Matthew He raises it on five occasions,[2] in Luke on no more than eight occasions,[3] whilst in John the word forgiveness does not appear at all. They affirm that when Christ made disciples He raised no theological problems with them. He simply called them to follow Him—no more. They insist that the Gospels make it very plain indeed that, for *Jesus*, salvation[4] and eternal life[5] consist in one thing, and in one thing only, a willing response to His unchanging summons, " Come, follow Me ! " This, they maintain, is the Gospel according to *Jesus*. They call upon the Church to have done with abstract issues and to attend to its practical task of following Christ.

The problem which this position raises is by no means abstract. It could not be more practical. The dilemma is simply this. We are called, without doubt, to follow Christ. But *we can't*. When we try to follow Him we find that we cannot do so. His standards are too high. Our resources are too low. The *kind* of following to which He calls—to love our enemies, to take up our cross, to hate our own lives—*this* is a following which is quite beyond our powers. It is easy to hold to the *theory* that the Gospel involves ' simply ' following Christ. The point at which the theory breaks down is the point at which we try to practise it.

He who believes that Christianity is first and foremost a matter of following Christ will sooner or later be forced to take one of two roads. He may so modify Christ's radical demands as to make them nothing more than reflections of his own poor principles—principles which

[1] Mk. 2: 5; 3: 28; 11: 25; 4: 12.   [2] 6: 12-15; 9: 2; 12: 31; 18: 21; 26: 28.   [3] 5: 20; 6: 37; 7: 47-50; 11: 4; 12: 10; 17: 3; 23: 34; 24: 47. [4] e.g. Lu. 9: 23-25; Mk. 13: 13.   [5] e.g. Mk. 10: 29, 30.

are sincerely held, no doubt, but which are *his* principles, not Christ's. He will take out of Christ's demands all that seems revolutionary or unreasonable, and he will follow whatever is left and he will call that ' following Christ.'

But there is another road which he may take. He may honestly face the fact that he *cannot* follow Christ, that Christ's uncompromising claims are simply too much for him; and then he will turn his back on Christ and try to follow Him no more. This was the road which the twelve disciples chose.

They had been called and ordained by Jesus. They had lived with Him for no less than three years. They had been given the inestimable advantage of receiving their training in discipleship at first hand from their Lord. At the height of His popularity, their frequent failures to follow in His steps [1] were tempered with some measure of success.[2] But, as soon as the element of opposition arose, their high resolutions were forgotten and they followed Him no more. They were ready to follow Christ in theory, to be sure— " Let us also go," said Thomas, " that we may die with Him." [3] ' " Though I should die with Thee," said Peter, " yet will I not deny Thee." Likewise also said all the disciples.' [4] But, in the Garden we see three men whom Jesus had relied upon to watch and to pray with Him in His hour of deepest need. We do not see them watching and praying. We see them fast asleep. Not once, nor twice, but three times in the evening. In the same Garden we see one of the Twelve, not following Jesus but betraying Him into the hands of His enemies. We see Peter, confronted at last with the chance to make good his grand protestations of loyalty; we see him shrinking from the road of discipleship, denying his Lord again and again and

---

[1] e.g. Mat. 16 : 23 ; 17 : 16 ff ; 14 : 30 ; Mk. 7 : 18 ; Lu. 22 : 24, 50.   [2] Lu. 10 : 17.   [3] Jn. 11 : 16.   [4] Mat. 26 : 35.

again. Finally, we see the whole band of 'followers' turning their backs on Jesus as they forsake Him and flee.

We doubt the disciples' sincerity as little as we doubt our own. But, for them, as for us, sincerity was not enough. With them, we hear the lofty calls to sacrificial living which ring through the Gospel story from end to end. But, in practice, lofty calls are not enough. With them, we see in Jesus an inspiring and exemplary picture of the noblest life which has ever been lived on earth. But neither inspiration nor example are enough. If we are to follow Christ we need nothing less than that which revolutionised the lives of the first disciples to the utter amazement of those who had known of their abject failure before Pentecost. We need that which, for the saints in every age, constitutes the very heart of the Gospel and which they proclaim as the explanation of their undeniably triumphant lives.[1] We need that which ushers into the world not merely great ideas and demands, but that which we can only describe as a new race of men, a new order of being, a new humanity.

It was to fashion this new humanity that Christ came into the world. This was the aim of His mission, of His Gospel. That Gospel, as we have maintained, had two deep notes. Two deep notes which, in the last analysis, blend into a perfect unity. The first note was the creative power of the forgiveness of sins. The second note was the gift of the life of God Himself to men.

The enormous practical significance of the forgiveness of sins can never be over-emphasised. The positive and creative power of forgiveness is man's greatest need. This is the fundamental fact which all the great religions of the world recognise and with which none of them,

[1] cf. Acts 12: 7 ff; 14: 19 ff; 27: 24 ff; 28: 3 ff.

not excluding Judaism,[1] is able to deal. None, that is to say, save Christianity. The best the non-Christian religions can do is to give advice regarding ways and means whereby man may, perchance, reduce his guilt before God. The uniqueness of Christianity, in this context, lies in the fact that God Himself deals with man's guilt—and that in the most radical, decisive and final way.

But there can be no doubt that the sense of guilt has been driven deep underground in the minds of multitudes of men. And there it lurks beneath the surface, causing a man to be wholly concerned with himself, either with the sense of guilt itself or, much more frequently, with attempts to justify himself and so to decrease the sense of guilt of which he is but dimly aware. His whole life is poisoned by his guilt. He is inextricably entangled in his guilt. He looks inward, always inward. He is closed in on himself. In the last analysis he sees none but himself. His world is no greater than the world of the babe in the womb.

Forgiveness pierces through his little world. It breaks wide a window to God. It makes the sinner fit for fellow-ship with God. It banishes the barrier of guilt. It opens up to his wondering gaze a vast world beyond. . . . a world in which he, a pardoned sinner, may live in deep communion with God.

In this experience he understands what Jesus meant when He said, " You must be born again." For he *has* been born again. Born into a world of whose existence he had never even dreamed—a world as different from the world whence he came as that world had been different from the womb.

Perhaps, had he been told how vast the difference was to be, he would have chosen to stay in the silent seclusion

---

[1] cf. H. R. Mackintosh, *The Christian Experience of Forgiveness*, Nisbet & Co., 1927, p. 19.

of the womb. He would have been alone with his guilt, to be sure, but he would nevertheless have been alone in a world which was small enough to permit his deceiving himself into believing that *he* was the lord of his confused, estranged world (the while he depended for life itself upon the life of the one in whose womb he lay). But now, when the birth-pangs of forgiveness have ceased, he finds that he has entered a great universe where *God* is Lord and he himself is no petty pantomime prince but a reconciled son of the living God, a man who lives in a wide new world where he is free from the dead weight of his guilt at last and all things—literally, all things—are made new.

He is *forgiven*!

The man-made barriers between God and his soul are down. His alienation from the holy God is past. By forgiveness he has entered, in the most realistic sense, into life-giving communion with God. In that communion, for the first time, he can begin to follow Christ.

We have likened the experience of forgiveness to the experience of human birth. The likeness is very close. For, as a child does not pass from the world of the womb into the great world beyond without pain and the shedding of another's blood, so the forgiven one is not born into this reconciled world without the wounds and the suffering of Another.

Now it is just at this point that we hear the loudest protests from those who believe that the Gospel is ' simply ' a matter of following Christ. For, in all good faith, they believe that the Church's doctrine of a forgiveness which comes through the Cross of Christ is something which has been added on to the straightforward record of the Gospels. Forgiveness through the death of

Christ, they insist, has no central place in the Gospels, and, above all, it has no central place in the thought of Jesus.

And yet precisely the opposite is the case. Jesus is quite explicit in linking forgiveness with His Cross. The subject of his death for sinners was constantly in His mind and very frequently indeed upon His lips throughout His ministry. It is of the first importance that this be understood.

We have already seen that the question of forgiveness is raised *explicitly* by Jesus on relatively few occasions. It is nevertheless true that the *idea* of forgiveness and the associated ideas of repentance and baptism appear at every turning point of the Gospel story. Christ insists that the reason for His coming into the world is ' to call sinners to repentance.' [1] Some of His most striking parables are explicitly concerned with the subject of repentance.[2] The burden of His earliest preaching is " Repent and believe the Gospel." [3] At Cæsarea Philippi He gives the disciples authority to forgive.[4] He sends them out to preach that men should repent.[5] And He sets the sacrament of baptism right at the heart of His Church's Gospel.[6]

Now, for Jesus, as we have maintained and as we shall shortly see, forgiveness was inextricably bound up with His approaching death. It was entirely dependent on the Cross. Forgiveness was the goal towards which His sufferings and death were directed. And the Gospel note of forgiveness dominates all other notes when it is heard, as Jesus sounded it, within the note of the Cross. Beneath and above all other notes this deep note is heard. Any serious study of the Gospels leads to the inescapable conclusion that the thought of His death dominated Jesus'

[1] Mt. 9 : 13. [2] Lu. 16 : 30; 15 : 7 f; 15 : 10; 15 : 11-32; Mat. 21 : 28 f.
[3] Mk. 1 : 15. [4] Mat. 16 : 19. [5] Mk. 6 : 12. [6] Mk. 16 : 16; Mat. 28 : 19.

mind and controlled His actions at least from Cæsarea Philippi to the end.

Again and again He impressed upon the disciples the fact that His whole ministry was moving towards the Cross. After Peter's confession 'He began to teach them that the Son of man must suffer . . . and be rejected . . . and be killed. . . . And He spake that saying openly.' [1] As they passed through Galilee 'He taught His disciples and said unto them, " The Son of man is delivered into the hands of men and they shall kill Him." ' [2] As they went up to Jerusalem 'He *again* took the twelve and began to tell them what things should happen unto Him, saying, " . . . the Son of man shall be delivered unto the chief priests and unto the scribes and they shall condemn Him to death and shall deliver Him to the Gentiles . . . and they shall kill Him." ' [3]

Christ insists not only on the absolute centrality but also on the *necessity* of His death. ' Jesus began to show His disciples that He *must* go to Jerusalem, and suffer much . . . and be killed.' [4] The thought of His death is constantly in His mind. When pressed to give a sign which would reveal His purpose He gives one which refers directly to His death.[5] He speaks of His burial.[6] He tells parables about His crucifixion.[7] He insists that the Scriptural prophecies concerning His death must be fulfilled.[8] Knowing full well that crucifixion awaited Him in the capital, ' He stedfastly set His face to go to Jerusalem.' [9] The death to which He went was a death which He was to *accomplish*[10]; it was a death which, from His point of view, He *ought* to suffer.[11] He insisted that it was ' for this cause,' the cause of death, that He had come

[1] Mk. 8: 31 f. [2] Mk. 9: 31. [3] Mk. 10: 32 f. [4] Mat. 16: 21, A.R.S.V.; cf. 26: 2; Mk. 9: 12; Lu. 13: 33; 17: 25; 22: 15, 37; 24: 26, 46; Jn. 3: 14; 6: 51; 8: 28. [5] Mat. 12: 38 ff. [6] Mat. 26: 12. [7] Jn. 10: 11 ff; 12: 24 ff; Mat. 21: 33 ff. [8] Mat. 26: 54, 56, 31; Mk. 14: 49. [9] Lu. 9: 51; 12: 50. [10] Lu. 9: 31. [11] Lu. 24: 26.

into the world.[1] Hence he deliberately entered the camp of His enemies; hence He refused to summon God[2] or man[3] to His aid when He was arrested; hence He stood silent throughout His trial, uttering no word in self defence. "The Son of man *must* suffer many things ... and be killed."

Not that He *wanted* to die. Unlike the Christian martyrs, He certainly did not rejoice in His death. "I have a baptism to be baptised with," He had said, "and how am I *straitened* till it be accomplished!"[4] In the Garden His anguish and terrible sense of dread are acute—"Father, save Me from this hour,"[5] He cries, and the sweat on His brow is like great drops of blood. And, being in an agony, He prayed more earnestly—"Let this cup pass from me!"[6] His awful sense of fear and dread was quite out of proportion to the physical sufferings which He was about to endure. Something was to happen on the Cross which could not be explained only by the blood and the nails. And Christ leaves us in no doubt as to what it was.

"This is My blood of the covenant," He said on the night on which He was betrayed, "which is poured out for many for the forgiveness of sins."[7] The death which meant everything to Him was directed towards one end and one end only—the forgiveness of sins. "This that is written," He went on, "must yet be accomplished in Me, 'He was reckoned among the transgressors.'"[8] As, in His Jordan baptism, He had reckoned Himself among the transgressors, so now, in the fullest sense, He was to identify Himself with sinners. His quotation from Isaiah 53 reminds us of the central theme of the chapter—

He was wounded for our transgressions,
He was bruised for our iniquities;

[1] Jn. 12: 7, 23-27. [2] Mat.26 : 53. [3] Mat. 26: 52. [4] Lu. 12: 50. [5] Jn. 12: 27. [6] Mat. 26: 39; cf. Mk. 15: 34. [7] Mat. 26: 28, A.R.S.V. [8] Lu. 22: 37.

The chastisement of our peace was upon Him,
And with His stripes we are healed—

it confronts us with the fact that Christ is here identifying Himself with the Suffering Servant whose sufferings are redemptive and representative, who suffers *on behalf of* the people, in order that the people may be forgiven. And finally we hear the crucial words, " The Son of man came . . . to give His life a ransom for many." [1] Forgiveness was to be achieved by the *substitution* (ἀντί, instead of) of His life for the lives of men ; He, in His own person, was to bear the whole weight of their sin and guilt. Small wonder that Christ prayed in *agony*. Small wonder that, by His whole demeanour, He communicated to His disciples the knowledge that an event of supreme significance was about to occur.

It is very difficult indeed to imagine how Jesus could have made the significance of His death more plain. Yet it is perfectly clear that not one of the disciples understood Him. But we are astonished at their blindness only to the extent that we ourselves fail to grasp the uniqueness of the Cross. That which was about to happen was so unprecedented an event that there was no analogy to which Christ might compare it. The reconciliation of the universe with its Maker was a task so vast as to defy man's understanding. The complexities of the gigantic problem reached high up into realms which man had never even envisaged and deep down into abysses of whose very existence man was entirely unaware. Something so big was to happen on the Cross that no finite mind could comprehend it.

Until it *happened*.

But, once it had happened, once the event had *become* an event, once it had become an event in the disciples' own

[1] Mk. 10 : 45.

experience—then the mystery of the Cross was a mystery no longer and the Church proclaimed Christ's death for sinners with one triumphant voice. The Cross, the disciples affirmed, was the root cause of the extraordinary transformation which had taken place in their own lives and which was taking place in the lives of the thousands of converts around them. In a multitude of different ways they sought to explain the inexplicable miracle of forgiveness. " You who were dead in trespasses," cried Paul, " God made *alive* together with Him (Christ), having forgiven us all our trespasses, having cancelled the bond which stood against us with its legal demands : this He set aside, nailing it to the Cross." [1] Christ's death had become, for Paul, the gateway to *life*. " . . . our Lord Jesus Christ who died for us that, whether we wake or sleep, we should *live* together with Him." [2] For the apostle, the guilt of the past was gone and a new world of freedom had come—" Christ gave Himself for our sins that He might *deliver* us from this present evil world." [3] This was the truth of the matter for Paul, the truth which had set him free.

And it was precisely the same overwhelming truth which had revolutionised the lives of all the other apostles. " (He) has *freed* us from our sins by His blood," cried John.[4] " Christ . . . died for sins," wrote Peter, . . . *that He might bring us to God.*" [5] And again and again the writer to the Hebrews strikes the same exultant note ; Christ's death is the ' new and living way ' which leads into the holiest place,[6] His death is a *deliverance* [7] for all who ' were subject to lifelong bondage.'

This is the note which sounds out continually in all the apostolic writings. One gains the impression that the wonder of forgiveness had burst in upon the apostles'

[1] Col. 2 : 13, 14, A.R.S.V.   [2] I Thes. 5 : 9.   [3] Gal. 1 : 4.   [4] Rev. 1 : 5,
A.R.S.V.   [5] I Pet. 3 : 18, A.R.S.V.   [6] Heb. 10 : 19, 20.   [7] Heb. 2 : 15,
A.R.S.V.

understanding like a bolt from the infinite blue, shattering all their preconceived ideas of God and sin and reconciliation, and opening up before them a vast new universe with limitless dimensions. They painted different pictures in an attempt to portray this one tremendous truth. But they knew well that the miracle of forgiveness could never be fully expressed in any picture. At the end of the day they stood silent before the Cross knowing that it proclaimed a truth which was more to be adored than analysed. And knowing too, that the bridge from the bondage of their former lives to the glorious liberty of their present experience was a bridge that had been built solely by the death of Christ upon the Cross. The Cross was not only the fundamental factor in their preaching. It was the fundamental reality of their lives. Whatever may be thought of the early Church's views about the meaning of Christ's death, it must never be forgotten that those views were held by men who had not only been impressed by the Cross but who had been *regenerated* by it. We may say that they were deluded. But we cannot deny that they were transformed.

Nevertheless, the Cross and forgiveness do not constitute the whole of the Gospel. Christ's mission does not end when men are reconciled to God. Forgiveness is *the bridge* to the life which God bestows ; but it is not the life itself. It is the fundamental reality which makes this life a possibility. But the supreme reality is *the life*.

Every sermon in the Acts of the Apostles calls upon men to repent and to receive God's forgiveness. But the overwhelming emphasis is on the life which God gives to those who are forgiven. For the early Church, Jesus was, above all else, ' the Author of *Life* ; '[1] the substance of

[1] Acts 3 : 15.

the preaching was 'all the words of this *Life*.'[1] God's gift was not only ' repentance,' it was 'repentance unto *life*.'[2] Forgiveness was the door by which men entered— by which men *continually* entered—into a sharing, by the activity of the Holy Spirit, in the resurrection life of Christ Himself. Hence, the greater part of the apostolic preaching was given to the themes of the Spirit and the Resurrection.

The apostles' testimony is ' to the resurrection of the Lord Jesus.'[3] Luke summarises Paul's preaching in the words, ' Jesus and the resurrection.'[4] Apart from the repeated references to the event [5] (which far outnumber references to the Cross), the resurrection is repeatedly declared to be the fulfilment of God's prophecies [6] and all the sermon illustrations are taken from Psalms which are held to foreshadow Easter Sunday.[7] It is hardly surprising that, when we read of the main impression which their preaching left on the minds of their hearers, it was that they ' preached through Jesus the resurrection from the dead.'[8]

Likewise they stressed the fact that this resurrection life was a gift of the Spirit of God. Peter explains the extraordinary change in the lives of the apostles as being the gift of the Holy Spirit.[9] Again and again we read that men are filled with the Holy Spirit, that they *receive* the Holy Spirit.[10] The Church was never content with the knowledge that men had reached the point of *believing*. That was not enough. The disciples were only satisfied when they knew that their converts had reached the point of *receiving*. The fact that great numbers of Samaritans had believed was a cause for rejoicing ; it was also a cause for

[1] Acts 5 : 20. [2] Acts 11 : 18. [3] Acts 4 : 33, A.R.S.V.; cf. 1 : 22; 2:24; 3 : 15; 10 : 41 ; 26 : 16. [4] Acts 17 : 18. [5] esp. Acts 2 : 14 ff; 13 : 26 ff. [6] e.g. Acts 13 : 26 ff. [7] Acts 13 : 33 : 34 : 35, etc. [8] Acts 4 : 2 ; cf. 17 : 32 ; 25 : 19. [9] Acts 2 : 17-21, 33. [10] Acts 4 : 31 ; 10 : 44 ; 13 : 52.

sending apostles to ensure that the converts might not only believe but that they might receive the life-giving Spirit of God.[1]

There is one early sermon, which, unlike all others, contains very slight references to the Holy Spirit and to the life which God imparts to believers. It ends on the note of forgiveness. But it ends at this point because the preacher is violently interrupted. We do not know whether or not he intended to go on and speak of the divine life which the Holy Spirit would impart. All we know is that the interruption is occasioned by the fact that the congregation *receives* this life by the gift of the Holy Spirit. ' While Peter was still saying this, the Holy Spirit fell on all who heard the word. . . .'[2]

This had been the ultimate reason for the Incarnation. "I am come," Jesus had said, "that they might have *Life*."[3] And now, in the experience of the infant Church, many of the parables and promises which had puzzled the disciples so much before Pentecost were seen to refer to nothing less than the gift of God's life to men. They recalled the parable of the leaven which was put into the meal and which permeated the whole of the lump until it was all leavened.[4] They recalled the parable of the Vine and the branches—"Abide in Me and I in you. As the branch cannot bear fruit of itself, except it abide in the Vine, no more can ye, except ye abide in Me."[5] They recalled the seed which was buried in the ground and which, entering into organic relation with the soil, grew up into a fruitful plant.[6] They remembered the words which had caused many of His disciples to ' walk no more with Him '—" He that eateth My flesh and drinketh My blood dwelleth in

[1] Acts 8 : 12-17; cf. 19 : 1 ff.   [2] Acts 10 : 44 f., A.R.S.V.   [3] Jn. 10 : 10.
[4] Mat. 13 : 33.   [5] Jn. 15 : 4.   [6] Lu. 8 : 4 ff and parallels.

Me and I in him."[1] And the words of His high-priestly prayer sprang to life—" I in them . . . I in them."[2]

Yet above and beyond all parables and promises, the apostles realised that the gift of union with God was the fulfilment of the whole life and ministry of Christ. They could never forget how, immediately before His ascension into heaven, Christ had enshrined this truth in the all-important sacrament of baptism. Having summarised the Church's mission in the command to ' make disciples of all nations,' He had instituted this sacrament whereby such disciples were to be received into His Church. The sacrament (which was a sign and a seal of the one Baptism of the Lord) was a baptism into the Name of Christ[3] and hence it was a baptism, through Christ, into (εἰς) the Name of the Father and of the Son and of the Holy Spirit.[4] The use of the word ' Name ' is of the greatest significance. E. V. Rieu, in his translation of John's Gospel, brings out the meaning of the word by substituting ' Being ' for ' Name ' —'. . . and that, believing, you may have life eternal in his Being.'[5] ' Holy Father, keep them in your Being.'[6] For the Hebrew, the Name certainly meant nothing less than the person himself. ' Yahweh Himself is present in His name,' writes Karl Barth.[7] ' Where the name, is there is the bearer of the name,' affirms Hans Schmidt.[8] To be baptised into the Name is to be made partaker in the life of Him into whose name one is baptised. Baptism ' into the name of Christ ' is baptism into union with the person of Christ. ' Being " baptised into the name of Christ," ' write the Church of Scotland Commissioners on Baptism, ' . . . means being baptised into Christ Himself, so that we are

---

[1] Jn. 6 : 56.   [2] Jn. 17 : 21 ff.   [3] Acts 8 : 16 ; Ro. 6 : 3 ; Gal. 3 : 27, etc.
[4] Mat. 28 : 19.   [5] *The Four Gospels*, Penguin Classics, 1952, p. 243 (Jn. 20: 31).
[6] *ibid.* p. 234 (Jn. 17 : 11).   [7] *Church Dogmatics*, I-1 (E.T.), p. 365.   [8] Quoted by K. Barth, *op. cit.*, p. 364 ; cf. A. B. Davidson, *Theology of the Old Testament*, T. & T. Clark, 1904, p. 36 ff.

grafted together with Him in a real and substantial union.' 'Union with Christ,' the Report continues, 'is the very heart of Christian baptism. Baptism is a grafting of the child or adult into the life of Christ, so that His life may overflow into the life of the baptised, regenerating it with the power of the resurrection.' [1]

This, as we shall shortly see, was the meaning of baptism for the apostles. It was so not only because their Lord had said that it was so, but also because participation in the life of Christ had become the greatest reality of their lives.

This, then, was the second deep note of the Gospel—union with Christ.

But it is precisely in the sacrament of baptism that we see that what, for the sake of clarity, we have called ' the two notes ' of the Gospel, are in fact *one* note. They are two sides of one reality. Baptism proclaims the forgiveness of sins through the death of Christ—' Buried with Him by baptism into death.' [2] Baptism proclaims the participation by the baptised in the life of Christ—' As many of you as have been baptised into Christ have put on Christ.' [3]

Forgiveness was accomplished by Christ so uniting Himself with men that, when He died, they died also—they died ' in His body on the tree.' But union with Christ did not stop at the Cross. It was an everlasting union. It was carried through into the Resurrection. If that had not been so there would have been no genuine union and certainly no genuine forgiveness—' If Christ be not raised your faith is vain ; ye are yet in your sins.' [4] But Christ *was* raised. And the humanity which had been united with Him in His death was now united with Him in His resurrec-

---

[1] *Interim Report of the Special Commission on Baptism*, 1955, Church of Scotland, p. 18.   [2] Ro. 6: 4.   [3] Gal. 3: 27.   [4] 1 Cor. 15: 17.

tion. 'If we have been united with Him in a death like His, we shall certainly be united with Him in a resurrection like His.'[1] That union which Christ had won with men in His life and in His death had struck the first and the fundamental note of the Gospel. But that note was only struck in order that the second and supreme note might be heard—the note of living union with Him. 'Christ . . . died for us *so that* . . . we might live with Him.'[2] 'We are buried with Him by baptism into death *that*, like as Christ was raised up from the dead . . . we also should walk in newness of life.'[3]

Hence, the whole Gospel was contained in the fact of baptism, in the fact of union with God. This was the fact which made all the apostolic writings ring with the note of triumph. This was the fact which had become the very breath of the disciples' lives. They knew what it was to be united with the living God and they proclaimed what they knew in no uncertain terms. "Do you not realise," demanded Paul of his converts, "that Jesus Christ is in you?"[4] "Your body is a temple of the Holy Spirit."[5] "You also are . . . a dwelling place of God."[6] "We are made partakers of Christ!"[7] proclaimed the writer to the Hebrews. And Peter affirms that his Christian brethren have 'become partakers of the divine nature.'[8] 'God's nature abides in him (who) . . . is born of God,'[9] writes John. 'We abide in Him and He in us.'[10]

It is not surprising that a Church with a life and a message like this swept the greater part of the Roman world into its ranks in a dozen generations. The disciples were not merely offering good religious advice. Nor were they merely calling men to sacrificial discipleship. They were living and proclaiming Christ's revolutionary Gospel—the

[1] Ro. 6: 5.   [2] 1 Thes. 5 : 9, 10, A.R.S.V.   [3] Ro. 6: 4.   [4] 2 Cor. 13 : 5, A.R.S.V.   [5] 1 Cor. 6 : 19, A.R.S.V.   [6] Eph. 2 : 22, A.R.S.V.   [7] Heb. 3 : 14.   [8] 2 Pet. 1 : 4, A.R.S.V.   [9] 1 Jn. 3 : 9, A.R.S.V.   [10] 1 Jn. 4 : 13, A.R.S.V ; cf. 5 : 20.

miracle not only of divine forgiveness, but the miracle of the life of God let loose in the lives of men!

To preach such a Gospel is *the heart* of the Church's mission. To materialise such a Gospel is *the body* of the Church's mission.

Now the heart of the Gospel stands in the same relation to the body of the Gospel as the Head of the Church stands to the Body of the Church. The one judges the other, reforms the other, gives life to the other. Set them apart and the end result is irrelevance and disaster. Unite them and the end result is a Church which has become the Body of Christ—inspired by His Lordship, possessed by His life, engaged in His purpose for the world.

CHAPTER SEVEN

YE SHALL BE FREE INDEED

THE CHRISTIAN ethic draws its life from the Person of Jesus Christ. That does not mean that it takes its stand upon the ' Life and Teaching of Jesus.' In the characteristic words of Paul Lehmann of Harvard, " If your ethic is based upon the life and teaching of Jesus Christ do not imagine for a moment that it is a *Christian* ethic." Such an ethic implies that everything that is essential for the Christian life happened *before* Christ was crucified and *before* He rose from the dead.

Yet that is precisely the ethic by which most of us order our lives. Which is to say that we live by Law. Our Law is called ' The Life and Teaching of Jesus.' It is, no doubt, the best Law of all. But it is no *more* than Law. It is unaffected by Good Friday and Easter Sunday.

We affirm that our great hope lies in Christ Crucified and Risen, but, so far as our daily decisions are concerned, that hope is of no account. We insist that Christ is no mere Teacher, not even the most exalted Teacher of all. And yet, for the ordering of life in the here and now, it is only as Teacher that we depend upon Him. There are many sincere men and women who, in the conduct of their daily lives, depend upon Jesus the Teacher but who do not claim Him as Saviour and God and Risen Lord. They hear us claim that the beliefs which they do not share with us make a radical difference to life. But they *see* no difference.

Often, there *is* no difference. We walk by the same Law as they. Small wonder that they regard our faith as irrelevant. What *we* do is done by the world and often done much better.

He whose conduct is conditioned only by ' The Life and Teaching of Jesus ' will often live a fine, unselfish, noble life. But the life which issues from the Cross and from the empty tomb is qualitatively distinguished from such a noble life, it possesses a radically different character, it travels in the diametrically opposite direction. Like the life of Him who rose from the dead it is a divine, recreative force which shocks and startles the world and raises a God-shaped query in men's minds.

Such a life is revelation. It is revelation because it is not only instructed by Christ's teaching, but also because it is revolutionised by the power and the immediate relevance of His Cross and His Resurrection.

To lose sight of this fundamental truth is to exchange the Christian ethic for a philosophical system shot through with a stronger or a weaker Christian strand. Such systems presuppose a harmony between man and God which, apart from Jesus Christ, simply does not exist. They are based upon man's nature as if his nature had not been judged and condemned by the Incarnation and the Crucifixion. They rely upon the wisdom of man and not upon the wisdom of God. They move, not from God to man, but from man to a god of man's devising. Hence, they are not signs of man's nobility but rather of his fall,[1] for they set man up in the place of God and judge all things in terms of him.

These systems are made up of laws or principles which are of universal application. (And the Decalogue and the Sermon on the Mount may be used in such a way as to be

[1] cf. F. W. Camfield, *Reformation Old and New*, Lutterworth Press, 1947, p. 88.

examples of such laws or principles.) They do not take into account the immediate historical situation in which men find themselves. They rule all concrete, temporal factors out of court. They subordinate people to abstract principles. Those who employ such systems tend to insist on the realisation of their principles without reference to the urgent needs of men. Their principles must overcome all the resistance which is offered to them by reality. The given situation is there to have these principles impressed upon it, if need be, by force.[1] They earn the protest of George Bernard Shaw, " You are so concerned with your principles that you are blind to other men's necessities ! "

But the Christian is not permitted to ignore other men's necessities for the sake of theoretical principles. He is not concerned with abstract ethics but with his neighbour and with God.

' Principles ' are the easy way out. They are like a bunch of impersonal keys with which to solve the problems of personal relations. We will not say that the Christian has no principles. But he is not *bound* by principles. ' Principles are only tools in God's hands, soon to be thrown away as unserviceable.' [2] If they remain in the hands of men they take on a demonic character. Hence God does not give man principles and leave him to work out their implications on his own. That would leave man master of the situation and the living God would become irrelevant.

This *living* God cannot be imprisoned in principles or in systems, no matter how severe and all-embracing they may be. Such systems may have an answer to every ethical question and yet avoid the one important question of God's relation with man. They enable man to hide away from

---

[1] cf. D. Bonhoeffer, *Ethics*, S.C.M. Press, 1955, p. 197.   [2] *ibid.* p. 8.

God. They alienate him from his Maker. They turn him from his neighbour to the rational good. They conceal him from himself. They satisfy his conscience—and he, his neighbour and his God are all the poorer for it.

Without such a system, the ' religious man ' is torn this way and that by all the unrelated instincts and desires which make up his fragmentary existence. He knows no inner unity or harmony. *With* such a system, his situation is ' improved.' His world is no longer atomised. It is only split in two.

On this level he is faced with two alternatives if his life is to have any semblance of inner unity. (But it will be no more than a *semblance* of unity.) The choice is between the transcendent and the historical. He may lose the transcendent in the historical process and concentrate his attention on his ethical life-in-the-world. Thereby he deprives the historical of any meaning at all for it is now unrelated to any absolute. Alternatively, he may centre his life upon the transcendent in such a serious fashion as to transcend absolutely the historical process. In this case, history loses all meaning.[1] It is not worthy to be compared with the absolute. But not only does history lose all meaning. The transcendent also loses its significance, for it has no form or content. Either way, man is torn asunder. If he chooses the world he loses God. If he chooses God he loses the world. For, so far as his ethic is concerned, God is God and the world is the world and ' never the twain shall meet.'

Yet they have met in Jesus Christ. They have been for ever united in Him. This is the heart of the Gospel. And that means it is the heart of ethics.

The ultimate condemnation of all man-centred systems

[1] cf. Reinhold Niebuhr, *An Interpretation of Christian Ethics*, S.C.M., 1948, pp. 150, 173.

of ethics lies in the fact that they stop short of Jesus Christ. If they say no more than, " Thou shalt not steal," they say that the Decalogue has the last word so far as conduct in the real world is concerned. The incarnation of God is quite irrelevant. If they go one step farther and base their system on the life and teaching of Jesus, we have seen that they do no more than multitudes of sincere non-Christians.

The tragedy of all those systems which have no relation to Christ Crucified and Risen is that they fail to come to grips with real life. They can do nothing about the fundamental problem of man's estrangement from God. They bring man to the point of cleavage between what he believes he ought to do and what he is able to do ; they bring him to this great wide gulf—and then they leave him there. There non-Christian ethics end. It is precisely there that the Christian ethic begins. The tension between the ideal and the real vanishes at the outset. The ought and the is are united in Jesus Christ.

Here we strike rock bottom. Here we have an answer to the question, " Where do we start our ethical pilgrimage ? On what fundamental reality do we base our lives ? " For the Christian, the answer cannot be in terms of systems, ideas or principles. It can only be in terms of Jesus Christ. We may not start with Christianity. Christianity is an abstraction. Nor may we start with God or with man. God and man are ideas. The only *real* man we know is Jesus Christ. And the only God we know is the God who became man. All else is unreality. The only reality we know is Jesus Christ.

It is for this reason that we do not have to *seek* after the Good. The Good has been actualised in the Person of

Jesus Christ. We do not have to seek after the answer to our ethical problem. It has been answered in Christ. In Him we find ultimate reality. He is the eternal God who has created, accepted, reconciled and made new the world. He is the one true man, bone of our bone and flesh of our flesh, tempted in all points like as we, and yet without sin. In Him the realities of God and of the world are no longer torn asunder. They are for ever united. Therefore we start, not with the conflict between a good ideal and hard reality, but with the accomplished reconciliation of the real world with the real God in the Person of Jesus Christ. That which was, in theory, incompatible, has found its final unity in Him. Hence, all ethical concepts which do not take Jesus Christ as their start point, are abstractions, they are unreal, illusory, irrelevant.

But in what sense does our ethic start in Christ?

It starts in Christ in that he who has been made a member of Christ's Body no longer needs to strive after his ethical goal. He has *arrived*. He has been *made* one with the ethical absolute, with Christ.

In the facts of the Incarnation and of the Crucifixion we see that God has accepted mankind. We see that His condemnation has fallen upon us, to be sure. But it has fallen upon us ' in such a way,' as Karl Barth insists, ' that what remains for us is the forgiveness of our sins.' [1] The condemnation and the forgiveness ' do not confront one another in a dialectical balance, but in a preponderance of the second over against the first.' [2] Christ's dying word was the word of forgiveness.[3] We are *forgiven*! We are at one with the Absolute.

In the fact of the Resurrection we see that this at-one-ment does not remain in the realm of theory. It has been corporealised in history. God has actually ushered in His

---

[1] *Kirchliche Dogmatik*, II, 2, 841.   [2] *ibid.* II, 2, 846.   [3] Lu. 23 : 34.

new creation in such a decisive way that the world has been visibly reconciled with Him in the Body of the Son.

Hence, our ethic is rooted, not in the uncertain future, but in the irreversible past wherein our humanity has *been* adopted and has *been* included in Christ's humanity. Therefore, our point of departure is the new humanity, the Body of Christ—it is the fact that we have been made for ever members of His Body.

The man who knows that this is true does not have to justify his deeds. He stands out in contrast with all who strive to follow ethical systems and who, in so doing, take up their stand as their own judge, as their own restorer. They carry their own justification in the guiding principle of their system. He who is a member of Christ's Body seeks no justification. He has *been* justified ! He takes his stand upon the Cross where he has been judged, condemned and *reconciled*. He is, therefore, a confident man. He sees what Luther came to see, that all does *not* depend upon *his* faith but on the merciful *God* who has justified him.[1] He does not strive to become righteous. He has been *made* righteous. All his unrighteousness has been swallowed up ' in the infinite abyss of the righteousness of God.'[2] Hence, if, in his choices, his decisions, his actions, ' consciousness of sin rush upon him . . . he believes that his sin is no longer his but Christ's.'[3] ' So that whatever Christ possesses, the believing soul may lay claim to . . . and, whatever belongs to the soul, Christ takes upon Himself as His.'[4] The Christian, in Luther's well-known phrase, is ' always a sinner, always a penitent, *always right with God*.'[5] *The* ethical decision is behind him. He cannot undo it. *God*

---

[1] *Weimarer Ausgabe*, 54, 179-187, quoted by Gordon Rupp in ' *Luther's Progress to the Diet of Worms*,' S.C.M., 1951, p. 33 f. ; cf. also Karl Barth's paraphrase of Ro. 1 : 17 in the *Römerbrief*—' The righteous shall live from *My* faithfulness,' O.U.P., 1933, p. 35 (2nd edition) ; cf. Gal. 2 : 20. [2] Luther, quoted by Rupp, *op. cit.*, p. 41. [3] Luther, *Select Works*, (Vol. I), Simpkin and Marshall, 1826, p. 26. [4] *ibid.*, p. 19. [5] G. Rupp, *op. cit.*, p. 54.

has made the decision that man is right with Him. That which is of primary importance is not that a man must commit himself to God—it is that God has committed Himself unreservedly to man.[1]

Therefore, in the realm of ethics—as in every other realm—the Christian man is free. His Lord was free, and he shares his Lord's humanity. He has been given the freedom of Christ. God has given that freedom to him and he *requires* him to live in that freedom. He is free from the anxiety and fear of living for himself. *God* has taken his life upon Him—his decisions and his very existence have their roots in the eternal God. With Luther, he may thankfully say, ' It is a great matter to be a Christian man, and to have a hidden life, hidden away, not in some place like a hermit, nor in his own heart . . . but in the invisible God Himself, and to live thus in the world.' [2] Such a man is no longer anxious as to whether or not he has done the right thing. God alone is his Judge. And His judgment has already fallen upon the One in whose Body he dwells. By God's grace, he is *in* the Body of Christ. Hence, he is *justified*. He is free to act boldly. No longer need he stand endlessly at the cross-roads, trembling lest he fail to take the right path. He is free to move forward. The right decision—God's decision—has been *made*.

It is here that we see that ethics springs from the heart of the Gospel. The Gospel and ethics are as united as inspiration and expiration. The Gospel says, " You are the Body of Christ." Ethics is that, " You *are*." The Christian ethic is not an imperative ethic. There is no grace in the ethic which cries, " Obey, because it is unlawful to resist!" [3] The Christian ethic is an *indicative* ethic. It says not, " You must ! " but " You *are* ! " This " You are ! " is the source,

---

[1] cf. T. F. Torrance, *Doctrine of Grace in the Apostolic Fathers*, Oliver & Boyd, 1948, p. 21.   [2] G. Rupp, *op. cit.*, p. 47.   [3] Calvin, *Institutes*, III, 8, 11.

the content, and the goal of the Christian life. " You are the Body of Christ ! " No matter how many errors we may make, no matter how faulty our doctrine may become, this fundamental truth stands fast—" No man shall pluck them out of My hand ! " [1]

Our point of orientation, as we have seen, is found in ultimate reality. It is found in Him in whom time and eternity meet, in whom heaven and earth are united, in whom God and man are one. We set out from this point, not in fear and trembling, but in peace and confidence because of what He has done in uniting us—and all our decisions—with Himself in His Body. But our ethical life does not consist only in a backward look, as though Christ were still on the Cross and we were still in His Body on the tree. It consists also in an upward look to the Christ who is the risen Lord of His Body, to the Christ who is alive and who has a *purpose* for His world.

In this situation, the Christian does not ask the usual ethical questions. He does not ask, for example, " How can I be good ? " [2] Such a question is doubly irrelevant. On the one hand, he is not good and never will become good. On the other hand, he has been made good, in Christ, in a final and an absolute sense. And, in any case, Christianity does not consist in his being good or in his being ' nice ' to people. Christ was not nice to people. He *loved* people with a deep, painful, sacrificial love which affirmed their humanity. There is a terrible ' Christian ' niceness which drains the man out of men. There is a conventional ' Christian' goodness which keeps men at arm's length from one another and which waters their red-blooded humanity down to a poor, pale sameness and leaves them with a

[1] cf. Jn. 10: 28.　[2] Bonhoeffer, *Ethics*, p. 55 ff. Throughout this section I am indebted to Bonhoeffer's brilliant study.

vague, other-worldly, ecclesiastical tinge. With such anæmic caricatures of the life in Christ the Christian spirit can never be satisfied and is compelled to rebel. " I'm not content with the goodness and niceness and duty which I have struggled for," exploded Florence Allshorn. " Now I want *Him*." [1]

Hence, the Christian no longer asks the familiar questions, " How can I be good ? How can I do good ? " Instead he asks the one question that matters, the only ethical question—" What is the will of the living Lord ? What is the will of God ? " [2]

The ultimate aim of ethics is not that I should be good or that the world should become good through my actions. ' Myself ' and ' the world ' are not ultimates. They exist only by permission of the one ultimate reality—the reality of the will of God.

That man who is primarily concerned with the problem of goodness, is concerned, in the first place, not with God but with himself. Hence, his response to temptation is sub-Christian and pitifully futile. He says, " This is wrong. The Bible says so." Or, " The Church says so." Or, " Christ says so." Not until he asks the liberating question, " What is the will of God ? " does the whole emphasis shift from man to God, from the weak and the transient to the strong and the eternal. No longer does he say, " I must not be angry. It's wrong." He asks, " What is the will of God ? " By that he does *not* mean, " What is the will of God concerning my anger ? Does God want me to be angry or not ? " Maybe He does. (' He looked round about on them with anger.') [3] The point of his question is, " How does God will this relationship to become creative and *real* in Jesus Christ ? " Only then is the whole atmo-

---

[1] J. H. Oldham, *Florence Allshorn*, S.C.M., 1951, p. 20.   [2] cf. Jn. 5 : 30; Mk. 3 : 35; Mat. 7 : 21; Jn. 6 : 38; 7 : 17; 4 : 34.   [3] Mk. 3 : 5; cf. Jn. 2 : 13-17 and Mat. 23 : 33.

sphere of his life transformed. No longer are his thoughts focused on himself and on his conduct; they are focused upon *God* and on His large purpose for His world. His first thought is no longer, " How can I gain the power to do what I ought to do ? " as though he *knew* what he ought to do. He does *not* know what he ought to do. Therefore, his first question is, " What is the will of God ? "

Dietrich Bonhoeffer has emphasised this point in his discussion of the Fall.[1] Man at his origin, he writes, did not know good and evil. He knew but one thing—God. In this knowledge of God he knew other men, he knew things and he knew himself. He knew himself as chosen and loved by God. He understood himself in the reality of his destiny—from the stand-point of creation, of the real, of God. Now the knowledge of good and evil, ' which seems to be the aim of all ethical reflection,' focuses, not on reality, not on God, but on man. Man knows himself apart from God. All his knowledge is based upon self-knowledge. In all things he sees himself. He understands himself in terms of his own possibilities, his possibility of being good or evil. *He* is the origin of good and evil. *He* is the one who chooses, not God. This is the reversal of all things. Man has become like God. *He* judges all things—himself, mankind and God—all with equal severity. Like the Pharisee, he may be the most ' ethical ' man in the world; his supreme concern may be with good and evil. And this concern only serves to emphasise his lostness. He lives in disunity—the disunity of the idea of good and evil.

By contrast, Bonhoeffer continues, *Jesus* lives in unity with God and with the world. It is for this reason that He and the Pharisees never meet. They are going in opposite directions. The Pharisees confront Him with man-made ethical problems based on the idea of good and evil. Jesus will not answer their problems. He refuses to be held by human alternatives. 'There is no single question put by men to Jesus which Jesus answers with an acceptance of the human either-or that every such question implies.' He is not confronted with a plurality of possibilities, but always and only with the will of God. The Pharisee is always faced with several possibilities. He *knows* that he has chosen the good. Jesus insists that His followers shall know nothing about the good they do. In the parable of the sheep and the goats, the sheep simply do not know about the good that they have done. They are far too concerned about freely doing the will of God. They are living in the unity of reconciliation with God. Their deeds are done without reflection on themselves or on the Good. They are aware of only one possibility—the will of God.

The *real* ethical question, therefore, centres around God's will. And this is no mystery. His will has been made manifest in the Person of the Son. The will of God is always to be understood in terms of Jesus Christ. The supreme question is this—" How is the reality of Jesus Christ operative in the world to-day and how does the Church and how do I participate in this reality ? "[1]

The great aim of the Christian, therefore, is, not to be good, not to change the world, not to imitate his Lord. His aim is *to be with Christ where He is*. That is the will of God.

But how do we become with Christ where He is and thus know the will of God ?

We become with Christ where He is when we realise, in the first place, that Christ is with us where we are. He is with us as Lord. Therefore, we no longer seek God's

[1] Paul L. Lehmann.

will from our own resources. We seek it from the one true source—from the Christ who is our Lord. But He must *be* Lord. We who would know the will of God must first allow the will of God to be accomplished in us. God requires one thing of us who would know His will ; namely, the faith in which we allow Jesus Christ to be our Lord. In that faith we become what Luther calls ' another man,' [1] and that process begins which J. S. Stewart describes as ' the unfolding of Christ's own character within the believer's life (which is) the essential relationship between religion and ethics.' [2] In this situation, the fact that Jesus Christ is the believer's Lord becomes the unifying truth about his life. And, knowing Christ as Lord, as the Lord who is with him where he is, the believer hears His voice directing him to the place where he may be with *Him* where He is.

Being with Christ where He is, his decisions are rooted solely in his knowledge of Him. He has, as Hendrik Kraemer affirms, ' one criterion—the new world, revealed in Jesus Christ ' ; he knows but ' one judgment, the judgment of faith, born from the new way of looking at all things and situations, through the faith in Jesus Christ.' [3] The direction of such a man's life has been completely changed. Now he is oriented not towards morality but towards revelation. That revelation is given only by the Christ who is his Lord.

It appears, then, that the Christian ethic has its roots in the Christian's membership in Christ's Body and in the

---

[1] *Select Works*, Vol. I, p. 13. [2] *A Man in Christ*, Hodder & Stoughton, 1951, p. 153. [3] *The Christian Message in a Non-Christian World*, Edinburgh House Press, 1947 p. 92. In this connection, as the author points out, the letters of Paul, John and Peter, constitute ' an inexhaustible mine of information from which can be learned how occupation with the trite but perennial problems of human life becomes the occasion for an amazing depth, freedom and sagacity of ethical decision, because all decisions emanate from the radically religious basis of faith.'

present Lordship of Christ. We must now ask the question
—" What of the Law and the Teaching of Jesus ? What is
their relevance for Christian living ? "

The first thing to be said about the Law is that behind
it and above it stands the Giver of the Law. The Law does
not exist by its own authority. It is neither static nor
impersonal. *God* gives the Law. It is not as though there
were God on the one hand and man on the other hand,
and, standing in between, separating man from God, the
independent Law. What there is, in fact, is God speaking
to man ; and His ever-fresh speech is heard in the Word
of the Law. This is a Word which reveals, supremely, the
nature of the Law-giver. It reveals His nature, not so much
as One who makes demands upon men, but as One who is
uncompromisingly *on man's side*. The Decalogue begins,
not with the word of prohibition, " Thou shalt not," but
with the word of inconceivable grace, " I am the Lord thy
God." We lose sight of this only when we tear the
Decalogue from its historical context. But *in* its historical
context we see that the Decalogue announces the fact that
God has committed Himself unreservedly to a particular
people ; He has bound them to Himself by His act of
self-commitment ; and He declares Himself to be the living
Lord who is active in their midst and who is working out
His historical purpose in them and through them—" which
have brought thee forth out of the land of Egypt, out of
the house of bondage." The Law is the gift of the living,
gracious, purposeful God.

The second thing to be said about the Law is that it
expresses the will of God. It expresses the will of the same
God who willed the Incarnation, the Cross and the Resurrection. His will does not change. It is renewed each day.
Hence the Law is not a static system, like the Law by which
the non-Christian world exists. *This* Law is an ever new

event in which God speaks His will into contemporary history. For example, the ' Thou shalt not kill ' becomes the creative, positive, living Law whereby the harsh, angry word which kills, and the fearful, unspoken word which kills with greater certainty, are transformed into the liberating word and look of reconciliation. It is in the realm of this event-ful Law that the believer will normally make his ethical decisions.

But there will be occasions—and if we were more sensitive to the need of our neighbour and more willing to hear the voice of God, would they not occur more frequently than they do ?—when the believer is confronted with a crucial decision to which the will of God, as expressed in the Law, gives no satisfactory answer. For example : what of the Polish refugee mother who was unacceptable as an immigrant because she was tuberculous, and whose healthy husband and children persistently refused to leave the refugee camp without her ? She broke the sixth commandment by committing suicide, and eight years of enforced idleness came to an end for her family; they were free to start life afresh in Canada. Or again : was the German generals' plot to assassinate Hitler, on 20th July 1944, contrary both to the Decalogue *and* to the will of God ? And again : who does God's will—the doctor who refuses to decapitate the unborn baby when its peculiar condition will lead inevitably to the death of both mother and child ; or the doctor who breaks the Law, kills the fœtus, saves the mother, and restores her to her remaining children ?

In such situations, the believer certainly does not ignore the Law. He considers seriously the limits which the Law sets to his action. But he does not separate the Law from its Giver. He remembers that the Christ who fulfilled the

Law is the ultimate reality towards which he is responsible. And he knows that Christ may set him free from the Law to carry out that deed which is necessary for the fulfilment of His purpose of reconciliation. In carrying out that necessary deed, however, the believer will not evade responsibility by hiding behind the will of God. He will stand erect in his freedom and will accept, in his own person, full responsibility for his deed. He will acknowledge the fact that he has broken the Law. But he will know that the One who has given him the freedom to break the Law is not only the One who created the Law but is also the One who forgives him if he becomes a sinner through obedience.

God is not imprisoned in His Law. He is free in relation to it. The reason behind His freedom is the fact that He is not *primarily* the Law-giver. He is, above all, the Creator. (His Name is Yahweh—' He that makes things to be.' [1]) His being Creator certainly involves His making laws. But the laws are *in order to create*. As Creator, He is supremely Creator of personal relations. And personal relations are of such a nature that, whilst they must grow in the sphere of law, yet they must not be bound by law.

There is no doubt that the Creator makes laws in the physical realm. But His first concern is not that the laws shall be kept. He has a *purpose* for His world and sometimes the laws obstruct that purpose. It is then that miracles happen. God makes laws in the realm of ethics. But, again, His first concern is not that everyone should observe the laws. He has a *purpose* for His people and sometimes the laws impede that purpose. It is then that He transcends the laws.

If we insist that God makes the Law and adheres rigidly

[1] Causative Hiphil.

to it, we are in danger of making the Law an idol and God a puppet—a puppet which we can handle. Like certain of the Pharisees, we can get round the Law. We can get ' God ' just where we want Him. And when that happens, we have lost God and have nothing but a lifeless legal system.

Let us underline the fact that the Decalogue *is* the sphere in which men must live before God, freely accepting His eventful commandment. But the Decalogue binds neither God nor man ; it does not limit the freedom to create. ' In obedience,' writes Luther, ' man adheres to the Decalogue. In freedom, man creates new Decalogues.' God gave His Law—" Thou shalt not kill." Yet He was to tell Israel to kill in the future—' Every man they smote with the edge of the sword . . . as the Lord commanded . . .'[1]—as He had told their father Abraham to kill in the past—" Take now thy son . . . and offer him . . . for a burnt offering."[2] The man who trusts God in such a situation is a man who believes that God has resources which are greater than His Law.[3]

It is from this background that we begin to understand the attitude of Jesus to the Law. " Till heaven and earth pass, one jot or one tittle shall in no wise pass from the law."[4] In this atmosphere Jesus lived. He honoured His father and His mother. He was ' subject unto them.'[5] And, in His last moments on the Cross, His concern was that His mother should continue to be honoured.[6] And yet, when this commandment stood in the way of the divine purpose, He did not hesitate to set it aside. He specifically grants His blessing to the man who, for His sake and for the sake of the Gospel, has actually *forsaken* his father and his mother—" There is no man that hath

[1] Josh. 11 : 6, 14 f.   [2] Gen. 22 : 2.   [3] Heb. 11 : 19.   [4] Mat. 5 : 18.
[5] Lu. 2 : 51.   [6] Jn. 19 : 27.

left . . . father or mother . . . for my sake, and the Gospel's, but he shall receive an hundredfold now in this time, . . . and in the world to come eternal life." [1] And His teaching goes one stage farther when He asserts, " I have come to set a man against his father and a daughter against her mother. . . . He who loves father or mother more than me is not worthy of me." [2]

Likewise, Christ approves the action of the disciples when they break the commandment to keep the Sabbath holy. He reminds the Pharisees that David and the priests themselves had broken the commandments before them. But His main concern is to point to His own personal sovereignty in relation to the Law—" The Son of man is Lord even of the Sabbath day." [3] Now the fact that Christ is greater than the Law means that He sometimes appears to the scribes and Pharisees as a subverter of the God-ordained ethical situation. According to the Law of Moses, the woman taken in adultery ought to have been stoned until she died.[4] Jesus lets her go without so much as a rebuke ! No doubt He makes an unequivocal demand— " Go and sin no more "—but that does not alter the fact that, in this concrete situation, He transcends the commandment and leaves the Law far behind. In the great parable on the nature of God the Father, the prodigal son is a man who covets his neighbour's goods,[5] who commits adultery,[6] and who can hardly be said to have honoured his father. And yet he is welcomed back into his father's house and is freely forgiven *before* he repents. If anyone receives Christ's condemnation in this parable it is the eldest son who claims that never, at any time, had he transgressed his father's commandment.[7]

It is not surprising if this attitude of Jesus leaves us

[1] Mk. 10 : 29.   [2] Mat. 10 : 35, 37 A.R.S.V.; cf. 15 : 4 ff.   [3] Mat. 12 : 8; cf. v. 6.   [4] Jn. 8 : 5; cf. Lev. 20 : 10.   [5] Lu. 15 : 12.   [6] Lu. 15 : 30. [7] Lu. 15 : 29.

with a disturbing sense of uncertainty in our ethical situation. It is impossible to tie Him down. As soon as we think that we have built up His teaching into a system, He breaks that system and our sense of insecurity returns. We believe, perchance, that at least we can rely upon the principle of unselfishness—" Give to him that asketh thee, and from him that would borrow of thee turn not thou away " [1]—and then we hear of five wise virgins who refuse to share their oil with those in need. *They* go into the Kingdom of God and those who had wanted to borrow from them are left outside in the dark. [2]

Let it be emphasised that Jesus insisted that His followers should take the Law seriously [3] and that they should take His own teaching even more seriously. [4] But His supreme concern was that men should take *Him* seriously. And that sometimes involved breaking the Law and transgressing His own commandment. [5]

We may not doubt that this is highly dangerous teaching. It lifts us out of the comfortable confines of the fulfilment of duty into the wide spaces of free, personal responsibility. It opens the door to anarchy—and that is why the world *must* live by Law. [6] It also opens the door to the Lord— and that is why the Christian *must not* live by Law. It is when we know that, in the last analysis, we are left in a thoroughly ' unsatisfactory ' position, with no unchanging, absolute principles, with no infallible ethical system, with nothing tangible to get a hold of at all—it is then that

---

[1] Mat. 5 : 42.   [2] Mat. 25 : 1 ff.   [3] Mat. 23 : 2 ff.   [4] " . . . but *I* say unto you . . ." Mat. 5 : 22, 28, 34, 39, 44 and Mat. 19 : 8 ff.   [5] Mat. 5 : 42 and 25 : 9. This explains Paul's attitude to the questions of fornication and things offered to idols in Corinth. He did not so much as mention the prohibitions of the Jerusalem Council (Acts 15 : 29), despite the fact that these very sins had been expressly forbidden in the decrees. He did the one thing needful by reminding the Corinthians that they were the Body of Christ and that they were indwelt by the Spirit. See Roland Allen, *Missionary Methods : St. Paul's Or Ours?* World Dominion Press, 1953, pp. 143 ff. *Spontaneous Expansion of the Church*, W.D.P., 1949, pp. 80 ff.   [6] ' The law is not made for a righteous man, but for . . . the ungodly and for sinners, for unholy and profane . . .' I Tim. 1 : 9.

we realise, for the first time, that we are left alone with God.

He who knows that he is left alone with God has become, not moral but mature. He has come of age. He has left the world of conventional ethics behind him and has entered a dimension in which that kind of ethics is simply not the point. The whole point of his life has become nothing less than the loving, reconciling, immediate purpose of the living God.

He therefore knows that the only serious ethical question is, " What is the will of God ? " At bottom, he knows one thing about the will of God. He knows that that will has been accomplished in Jesus Christ. He therefore knows that that action is in harmony with the will of God which is in harmony with his living Lord. His action is in accordance with God's will as it bears witness to and mirrors the present action of Jesus Christ in contemporary history. In other words, the right action does not spring from a shrewd assessment of the possibilities before him, but from such an orientation of his life towards the Person of Jesus Christ as results, concretely, in the doing of God's particular will and the fulfilment of His particular purpose in His world to-day.

This ' orientation ' is seen most clearly in the celebration of the Eucharist. At the Lord's table the believer has the unshakable conviction that here the will of God is being done. Here he believes that, by Christ's broken Body, he who is not right with God has been *made* right with God. He knows this to be God's will. In accepting the bread and the wine he accepts what God has done for him as right. He accepts the fact that he is condemned and *reconciled* and now stands in the freedom with which Christ has made him free. This freedom is the freedom to be a man before God—really to be a man. A man with his own action and with his own unique humanity.

Living thankfully in this freedom, he covets it for others. He knows that *that* is the will of God. At the table he receives the nature of his Lord and is thereby enabled to act towards others in the stead of Jesus Christ. His action becomes Christ's action. It does not only have the form and the power of Christ's action. It *is* Christ's action. As Christ stands beside him, just as he is, affirming his humanity, so he stands by his neighbour, just as *he* is, affirming *his* humanity. This is no ordinary ' standing by.' It is a ' standing by ' in which the new humanity of Jesus Christ gains a fresh foothold in the world and in which God's eternal purpose is realised.[1] It is a ' standing by ' through which my neighbour becomes a man before God.[2] A *man*! Before *God*! This, the believer knows without question, is the will of God. It was for this reason that Christ came into the world. This action is, therefore, the only real ethical action. It is purposive, ultimate action. It is part of creation.

[1] cf. the Countess in Christopher Fry's ' *The Dark is Light Enough* ' of whom it was not only said that ' Lives make and unmake themselves in her neighbourhood as nowhere else,' but also, ' There are many names I could name who would have been remarkably otherwise except for her divine non-interference.' O.U.P., 1954, p. 5.   [2] Eph. 4 : 13 A.R.S.V. ' . . . until we all attain . . . to mature manhood.'

CHAPTER EIGHT

A NEW CREATION

WHEN ATHANASIUS insisted that Christ 'was made man that we might be made divine,'[1] he did no more than underline the apostolic affirmation that, by virtue of the Incarnation, Christians are 'partakers of the divine nature.'[2] But it is at this point—the point at which we stop speaking in general terms and begin to make the application in very personal terms—it is at this point that the whole of our theological position is challenged.

It is one thing for us to affirm that *the Church* is the Body of Christ. It may be quite another thing for us to affirm that the *believer* shares realistically in the life of Christ. 'The Church as the Body of Christ' may be nothing more than an abstract idea. But 'the Christian as partaker in Christ's nature'—this is something which comes out of the abstract and into the concrete. It is theology particularised in my flesh and blood. And should it be that I discover that I do not believe this latter affirmation, I suddenly perceive that I do not believe the former either.

"I am the Vine, ye are the branches. Abide in Me and *I in you*."[3] "The glory which Thou gavest Me I have given them . . . *I in them* and Thou in Me . . . that the love

---

[1] *De Incarnatione* 54 : 3.   [2] 2 Pet. 1 : 4; cf. Jn. 1 : 12; 1 Jn. 3 : 2.   [3] Jn. 15 : 4, 5.

wherewith Thou hast loved Me may be in them and *I in them*." [1] If the testimony of Jesus were limited to such significant statements as these we would find it difficult to dismiss the claim that He intends the believer to share in His life. But the testimony with which we are confronted is one which has its source in everything we know of Christ's Person. It begins with His birth and continues beyond His resurrection. It is that testimony with which we have been concerned throughout this study, namely, the testimony of the whole movement of the Incarnation. By His birth, throughout His life, in His death and resurrection, Jesus is engaged in uniting Himself with men. Not with Man in the abstract but with *men*, with persons of flesh and blood. We know that He did not descend from heaven merely to outline a pattern of life for man or to give man a new orientation. He came to bring *the life of God* into the lives of men—*real* men. For this He lived and suffered and died—for this and for this alone.

And that is why the record of the early Church throbs with a life that is astonishingly new. The branches pulsate with the life of the Vine. And apostles and martyrs explain the miracle in no uncertain terms—" I live," cries Paul, " yet not I, but *Christ liveth in me*." [2] And, turning to the wavering disciples in Galatia, he says, " My little children, of whom I travail in birth again until *Christ be formed in you*." [3] And, to those who are strong in the faith, he prays " That Christ may dwell in your hearts by faith . . . that ye might be filled with all the fulness of God." [4] And again he prays that " God would make known what is the riches of the glory of this mystery . . . which is *Christ in you* [5] . . . *Christ who is our life*." [6]

[1] Jn. 17: 22, 23, 26; cf. Mt. 10: 40.   [2] Gal. 2: 20.   [3] Gal. 4: 19.
[4] Eph. 3: 17, 19.   [5] Col. 1: 27.   [6] Col. 3: 4.

'This life into possession of which souls entered by conversion,' writes J. S. Stewart, ' was nothing else than the life of Christ Himself. He shared His very being with them.'[1] "There is a new creation whenever a man comes to be in Christ."[2] 'It is καινότης ζωῆς, a new quality of life, a supernatural quality.'[3]

This is the life which cuts across Church frontiers and which judges and condemns the sinful divisions within the one Body. It unites all who have been led by Christ through the outer trappings of religion into the very being of God Himself. 'Religion is a divine life,' writes Henry Scougal, the Episcopalian, '. . . God dwelling in the soul and Christ formed within us.'[4] 'It is an union of the soul with God, a real participation in the divine nature.'[5] The Roman Catholic, Dom Columba Marmion, affirms, ' The Divine Plan consists in calling the human creature to participate . . . in God's own eternal life.'[6] And Thomas Kelly, the American Quaker, plumbs the depths of the Christian life when he declares, ' The substance of (Christ's) body becomes our life and the substance of His blood flows in our veins.'[7] ' Christ and all He has is given to us,' writes Luther, ' Christ and the soul become one flesh.'[8]

When ' Christ and the soul become one flesh,' there can be no doubt that the purpose of the Incarnation is being fulfilled in the life of the believer. The whole work of Christ is being perfected in the life of one for whom He became man. In this union with Christ, a new creation—literally, a new creation—is ushered into the world. A real *person* is born. The new humanity of Jesus takes flesh and

---

[1] *A Man in Christ*, Hodder & Stoughton, 1935, p. 193.   [2] 2 Cor. 5: 17, Moffatt.   [3] J. S. Stewart, *op. cit.*, p. 193.   [4] *The Life of God in the Soul of Man*, Westminster Press, 1948, pp. 33-34.   [5] *ibid.*, p. 30.   [6] *Union with God*, Marmion's letters of direction by Thibaut; Sands & Co., 1934, p. 1.   [7] *A Testament of Devotion*, Hodder & Stoughton, 1943, p. 69.   [8] Gospel Sermon, Lenker's edtn. of *Luther's Works*, Vol. 12, 16.

blood in a miraculous, unique and never-to-be-repeated event.

A *person*, we say, is born. Hitherto, the man has been an individual—an isolated individual. Having no relation with Christ the Mediator, he has no real relation with other men. He does not know that such relation exists. For him, to use the language of Martin Buber, all things, including men, have been objects to be used and experienced. He has been inhabiting the world of It, of separation. He knows nothing of the world of Thou, of relation. He ' remains a functional point, experiencing and using . . .', fleeing into ' the senseless semblance of fulfilment, . . . groping in a maze and losing (himself) ever more profoundly . . . He is wholly and inextricably entangled in the unreal.' [1] Such a man is terribly alone. He has never *met* another man. And, having no relation with either God or man, he does not know what life is for. And so he exists, or rushes vainly on, in the world of action, of ideas, of ' religion '—a separate, a tragically separate individual.

But now, in union with Christ, he *becomes*. He becomes a *person*. A person who, being united with the Mediator, lives in relation with all men. For Christ has relation with all men. As a person, the believer addresses all men as Thou, He *meets* each Thou. And he knows that each Thou leads him beyond to the eternal Thou. His whole being is involved in this becoming. It is not merely his ' religious ' self which has adopted a new set of symbols. Where once there were several selves there is now one self, one authentic person. Being partaker in the wholeness of Christ, he has himself been made an effective whole. He is therefore able to distinguish between that which partakes of the wholeness of God and that which exists in the fragmentariness of the

[1] *I and Thou*, T. & T. Clark, 1950, pp. 64, 70, 61.

passing age. He is free from capitulation to the multiple pressures of the society in which he lives. He is free from anxiety over the praise or blame of his fellows. He is free with the freedom of the Christ with whom he is one. For now he apprehends all things with the eyes of Christ. ' We have the mind of Christ.' [1] In the most profound sense he has begun, in Christ, to grasp the whole nature of things. He has 'a feeling of intimacy with the inside of the cosmos.' [2] He has become what George Fox called ' an established man.'

Such an ' established man ' is really *alive*. Unlike the world about him, he is not obsessed with action. He knows that his first task is to *live*. He knows that it is not his instruments or his institutions which count, but *himself*— for *he* is God's instrument.[3] Therefore, his primary duty is not, for example, to engage in political or social action; neither is it to produce blue-prints for evangelism. He is aware of the fact that God breaks through into history not so much through programmes as through people—people who are alive with the life of Christ. Therefore, his supreme concern is to know who he is—one in whom the living God abides. And his first task is to *be* who he is. To live, really to live, the life of God. Action—the *right* action— will follow on being. The man who does not share in the life of God will never perform this right action. He will act, to be sure. But his action will be fruitless, like the action of a galvanised puppet. The established man acts creatively because he is *alive*.

Whence comes this life ? Fundamentally, it has its roots in the presence of Christ in the believer. Christ is the sole source of life.[4] And sharing in His divine-humanity

[1] I Cor. 2 : 16.　　[2] Justice Holmes, quoted by Kelly, *op. cit.*, p. 12.　　[3] cf. Jacques Ellul, *The Presence of the Kingdom*, Westminster Press, 1954, p. 80. [4] Heb. 1 : 1-4.

produces certain radical changes in the whole being of the Christian. To understand the nature of these changes is to understand something of the nature of the life which Christ produces in the believer. We may outline the changes thus.

The primary change consists in an awareness of God as *God*. The man in whom Christ dwells cannot be unaware of God's presence—His *real* presence. For this awareness there is no substitute. Neither a Christian pattern of life, nor a noble religious ethic, nor a Christocentric theology can be any substitute for an awareness of God.

All other kinds of awareness leave me unchanged in my innermost being. They change my conduct, to be sure. But they change it for the wrong reasons and from the wrong motives. And hence my conduct lacks unity, freedom, spontaneity, creativity. It is my *conduct* which is changed, not *me*. Awareness of *God* involves a conversion, a total re-orientation of all that I am around the holy One. My whole *being* has been invaded by God. *He* lives in me. And I live, as it were, in a new atmosphere whose vitality and content is God Himself. As a bird in flight, if suddenly deprived of air, would both die and fall to the earth—so with my soul and God. He is both the source of my life and the ground of my existence. As I partake in His life I find that I inhabit a new Kingdom. I am inhabited by a new King. I become a stranger and a pilgrim in the world. My presuppositions and my responsibilities are determined by Him who dwells within me. Like the king's ambassador who lives on foreign soil, I live and labour in one country but my standards, my hopes, my resources and my conduct are determined by the country, by the One, to whom I belong.[1]

[1] cf. Ellul, *op. cit.*, 45.

Such awareness of God creates life. But it does not lighten life. Rather it makes life heavy, heavy with meaning. Heavy with God. The man who, with Thomas à Kempis, ' carries everywhere about with him Jesus his Comforter ' [1] knows not only ' the great grace of *union* with God ' [2] but the great grace of union with *God*. And ' it is a fearful thing to fall into the hands of the living God.' [3] He who, like Frank Laubach, knows days when he ' lives wrapped in God, trembling to His thoughts, burning with His passion ' [4] is aware that God's presence burns deep. ' For our God is a consuming fire.' [5] The presence of God, the presence of the Word, burns, as it were, into his heart and into his very bones,[6] until his whole being is penetrated by God. And he lives his life, he conducts his daily affairs, in unceasing awareness of God. Now strong, now weak, but never altogether absent, this awareness charges each moment with worship. He is no longer primarily concerned with developing means to achieve an end. He carries God's end within him. And God's means and His end are identical—Jesus Christ the Lord.[7] Where Christ is present, the Kingdom is come. And Christ dwells in his heart. Of this he is profoundly aware. It is this awareness that conditions all he does and all he says and all he is.

He who, in Calvin's words, ' is become one substance with Christ,' [8] and who is ' united into one body with Him,' [9] has about him an atmosphere of unconditional acceptance. It is precisely that atmosphere which surrounded Christ, which both attracted and repelled men, and which was only recognised for what it was by supernatural

[1] *Imitation of Christ*, Bagster & Sons, p. 124. [2] *ibid*., p. 261. [3] Heb. 10 : 31. [4] *Letters by a Modern Mystic*, Student Volunteer Movement, U.S.A., 1952, p.15. [5] Heb. 12 : 29. [6] Jer. 20 : 9. [7] cf. Ellul, *op. cit*., p. 80. [8] *Inst*. 4 : 17 : 3. [9] *ibid*., 4 : 17 : 11.

powers—" I know Thee who Thou art, the Holy One of God ! " [1] This was the atmosphere which brought men running to Jesus and which to-day, far more than institutions and techniques, brings men running hopefully to those in whom He dwells.

This atmosphere finds expression in the fact that the believer is *open* to all men. He has *time* for all men. He *exposes* himself in freedom and in love to those whom the world calls good and bad, high and low, but whom he calls " my brethren." He is at home in the presence of the mighty, for he is at home with the mighty God. He is at home in the presence of the lowly, for he, a lowly sinner, has been welcomed home by God. He is not ashamed to welcome holy men for he has welcomed the Holy Man. Neither is he ashamed, with St. Francis, to embrace the blasphemous leper and to kiss his sores ' all rotting and stinking,' [2] for he, despite his baseness and uncleanness, has been freely embraced by the infinite God. He has been *accepted* in the Beloved. He is therefore able to *accept*.

This atmosphere, then, has its source in the fact that the believer is himself unconditionally accepted by God. It is important for us to emphasise the fact that it is the *believer* who is accepted. In this respect, it is not *Christ* who is accepted but it is the sinful believer. Undoubtedly Christ *is* accepted and the believer is himself accepted *for the sake of* Christ. But God does not, by a legal or an ' optical ' fiction, see only *Christ* when He forgives the sinner. He sees the *sinner* with all his sin. And it is the *sinner* whom He accepts. God does not accept a phantom, an ' ideal ' man existing only in the sinner's imagination. He accepts the sinner—bad temper, lust, envy, pride, self-seeking—God accepts him all. For Christ came into the

---

[1] Mk. 1 : 24 ; cf. 1 : 11 ; Mat. 8 : 29 ; 17 : 5.   [2] *Little Flowers of St. Francis*, Everyman, 1947, pp. ix, 45.

world not to save that which is *righteous* in me.[1] Nor yet that which is only *sinful* in me. He came to save *me* !

Now the fact of God's total acceptance is of supreme importance, for only the man who has squarely faced this fundamental truth is free to become a real person. If he believes that only a part of him (the ' good ' part of him) is accepted by God, he is obliged to pretend to be someone other than he is. He lives in unreality. He is trapped in a world of make-believe unless he is accepted, and unless he accepts himself, as he really is. It is not until a man knows that he—really *he*—has found unconditional acceptance with Almighty God, that it becomes possible for the life of God within him to deal effectively with his sin. When the ' bad ' child is rejected by his family, he has no alternative but to go from bad to worse. But, if he knows that, despite his sin, he is fully accepted by his family, he is, for the first time, free to reform. His sin can be healed by love. He no longer has to *hide* from his sin.

But most of us hide from our sin. We make-believe it is not there. We pretend that we are the people—the insubstantial ghosts—which we, in our folly, would *like* to be. Or, worse, we pretend that we are the people whom our friends would like us to be (or whom we *imagine* our friends would like us to be). We inhabit a dream world. And, hence, we never *live*. We are never ' *us*.' We do not dare to be ourselves. For we know that there is evil in ourselves. And we are afraid of evil.

But there is One who is not afraid of evil. He has conquered it once for all. He is the Christ who is one flesh with the believer; the Christ through Whom Almighty God freely accepts the believer. And hence the miracle comes to pass that, being possessed by the fearless Christ, the believer loses *his* fear. He lives without fear.

[1] 1 Tim. 1 : 15 : Mat. 9 : 13.

Without fear! His *atmosphere* is different from that of other folk. He generates peace as before he generated dispeace. His spirit is one of acceptance as before it was one of fear. Here is the leaven in the lump, the indefinable quality which makes us envy certain people and not know why we envy them. They are unafraid. And to be unafraid is to be alive. Alive with the life of Christ—a life which generates the spirit of forgiveness, an atmosphere of unconditional acceptance. For the sinner who is wholly accepted by God discovers a creative spring of ' acceptance ' welling up from the Christ within.

He has become a *creator*. Not so much by what he *does* as by what he *is*. Wherever he goes, he fashions a new world, for he lives in the forgiveness of sins, and it is the forgiveness of sins which makes all things new. He waits eagerly to forgive. To be sure, he does not *speak* forgiveness. No hint of ' holy pardon ' clouds his relations. The other does not know that he has been *forgiven*. But he knows that he has been *accepted*. And accepted in so complete and personal a fashion as lifts his thoughts in wonderment to God.

Nor is the fruit of forgiveness limited to the one who is forgiven. It enlarges the spirit of him who forgives. He is released from the bondage of resentment and self-pity. The burden of hate falls from his back. He has found a freedom which is not of this world. He is free with the freedom of God !

Nor is his freedom confined to his relations with his fellows. He is free in relation to God. He has entered into a large place where he knows more and more of the length and breadth and depth and height of God's acceptance, God's forgiveness—for at last he is able to pray with sincerity : " Forgive us our trespasses *as we have forgiven* (ἀφήκαμεν) those who trespass against us." More and more deeply he enters into the forgiveness of God. More and more radically he finds acceptance with God. More and more completely he receives a holy freedom which embraces his Maker, his neighbour and himself in a creative unity.

The extraordinary creative power of forgiveness has its explanation in the nature of the One who forgives. And supremely in His nature as *love*. He is the God of forgiveness because He is the God of love. Undergirding the divine acceptance is the divine ἀγάπη. God forgives the sinner because His love is greater than the sinner's sin.

It is a profoundly disturbing experience to come to the realisation that one is loved by God. For the love of God is an intensely personal love. It is what the Old Testament calls a ' jealous love.' It is the love of the Shepherd out on the hill-side seeking a single sheep. It ' chooses one object among thousands and holds it fast with all the strength of its passion and its will, brooking no relaxation of the bond of loyalty.' [1] It is an exclusive love. It calls me by my name. *God* calls me by my name ! His love— *His* love—embraces *me* !

This love, the love of God, is expressed in *relation* with the beloved. God meets the beloved face to face. He has communion with the beloved, entering into deepest relation. [2] Where there is love there is a giving of *oneself*. One's whole life enters into this ' giving.' In such a manner God, in the fulness of His being, comes to me personally, ' choosing one among thousands ' (and I—yes, *I* !—am that ' one '), and enters into relation with me ! The Eternal One breaks through the veil and enters into my human flesh. Eternity breaks through into time.

And that ' time ' is always *present* time. No doubt God's love was revealed on the Cross ; no doubt it will

[1] Quell & Stauffer, *Love*, A. & C. Black, 1949, p. 32.   [2] Gen. 4: 1.

be perfectly expressed in heaven. But it is to be lived in *now*. God, the living God, loves me *now*. The Lord, the Creator of the ends of the earth, loves me personally now ! Each moment of my life is charged with eternal significance. The everlasting God is present, not only to Humanity, but to *me*. " Whither shall I go from Thy Spirit ? or whither shall I flee from Thy presence ? " [1] The thought of this ever-present, ever-loving God would fill us with a proper terror did we not understand the infinite tenderness, the patience and compassion of the One whose glory we behold in the face of Christ. It is the love of Christ—the Christ who wept over Lazarus—it is *His* love, it is *He* who continually approaches us. *His* love, the love of God, embraces us.

Something decisive happens to the man who knows that he has been embraced by the love of God. He can never be the same man again. It is not only that He becomes aware of the fact that he, personally, matters. The supreme reality in this situation is that, having been embraced by the love of God, he has been made partaker in God's nature. For God's nature is love. And God's love has been unconditionally given to him—to *him*, in the most particular way. It has penetrated the very springs of his being. And he stands erect in all his newfound humanity —accepted by God, loved by God, partaker in God's nature as love.

Now this ' partaking ' is what gives substance and power to the life of the believer. This is what lies behind the ' atmosphere of unconditional acceptance.' This atmosphere has its roots in the love of God which has been imparted to him. It has its fruits in his love for men and, more fundamentally, in his love for God.

He *loves* God. And he knows that his whole life is

[1] Psa. 139 : 7.

dependent upon the God who loves *him*. He has nothing to fear. He rests securely and confidently upon God. He leaves all ultimate responsibility to God. He cuts loose every bond except the bond of love which God Himself has given. God has become his Beloved, his Holy Beloved, his life.

His love for God, God's love for him, is that which changes all things. And especially does it change his relations with his fellows. Being partaker in God's love, he loves his brethren. Like the love of God, his love for them is a jealous love. He is not so much concerned to love the world at large as to love the man beside him; to love him as a particular person; to love him by name; to love him with the same unreasonable love with which God loves *him*. Such a love wells up instinctively within him, for it arises from the divine love which has been given to him. It is as irrational, as inexplicable and as irresistible as the love of Christ upon the Cross. For it *is* the love of Christ upon the Cross.

The believer expresses this love to all men—literally, to all men. In the light of the love which God has imparted to him and which gives him relation with all, *every* man without exception is an object for his love. ' The hard lined face of the money-bitten financier is as deeply touching to the tendered soul as are the burned out eyes of miners' children, remote and unseen victims of his so-called success.' [1] With Kagawa he cries to every man, " My heart is wide open for you. Restraint ?—that lies with you, not with me. And for your souls I will gladly spend my all and be spent." [2]

Here, then, is the source of the believer's extravagant love. He is accepted by God. He is loved by God. He

---

[1] Thomas Kelly, *op. cit.*, p. 82. [2] *Love the Law of Life*, S.C.M. Press, 1934, p. 89.

is made partaker in God's love. He is rooted and grounded in God's love. And, hence, he comprehends, with all the saints, the immeasurable character of the love of Christ which reaches out, through him, to his brethren in unconditional acceptance.

The man who has become a person through his union with Christ, is a man who stands in holy awe of God. God is not only his familiar, loving friend. He is also the sovereign God beyond. ' Am I a God at hand,' saith the Lord, ' and not (also) a God afar off ? '[1] There is a profound sense in which he fears his God. ' The fear of the Lord,' said Job, ' *that* is wisdom.'[2] And this fear arises especially when a man thinks of God's love for him. That God—really *God*—loves *him* . . . That God is, at this particular moment, as I sit in this chair, seriously and personally loving *me*! That His love, God's love, gives Him a total, penetrating concern for all that I am and do at this moment, and for all that I shall be and shall do every moment of my life! If this does not make me afraid, then I do not know who this God is of whom I speak. Perhaps He is my toy,[3] my plaything, my God-on-the-shelf, the God whom I have made in my own image. But if He is *God*, ' the high and lofty One that inhabiteth eternity, whose name is Holy,'[4] what can I do but fall down before Him as the young Isaiah fell down, crying, "Woe is me, for I am undone . . . for mine eyes have seen the King, the Lord of hosts."[5]

I am afraid of God because He is *God*. He is קָדֹשׁ, holy, separate, removed. If He would *remain* removed, my fear would take a different form.[6] But He does *not* remain removed. He, the Lover, continually approaches me. He

---

[1] Jer. 23 : 23.   [2] Job. 28 : 28.   [3] Isa. 44 : 17, 20.   [4] Isa. 57 : 15 ; cf. 40 : 23, 25.   [5] Isa. 6 : 5.   [6] Contrast Mat. 28 : 4, 5, 8.

refuses to forsake me. 'If I take the wings of the morning and dwell in the uttermost parts of the sea; even there shall Thy hand lead me, and Thy right hand shall hold me.'[1] The hand of *God* shall hold me! And 'It is a fearful thing to fall into the hands of the living God.'[2] So long as our God is dead or afar off we know no such fear. But as soon as He becomes, for us, the *living* God, the *present* God, we are afraid.

When God revealed Himself to Moses on Sinai in thunder and lightning and fire and the voice of a trumpet, Moses said "I exceedingly fear and quake."[3] And he was *right* to fear. His was the same fear that we see in the disciples on another mountain, when they caught a glimpse of the glory of the living God in the transfiguration of Jesus. 'They fell on their face and were sore afraid.'[4] It was the same fear that we see in all the disciples when, after the resurrection, the holy God revealed Himself to them in the upper room. 'They were terrified and affrighted.'[5]

This proper fear inevitably follows the knowledge that the holy God is at work in our lives. 'Work out your own salvation with fear and trembling for *God is at work in you* . . .'[6]

This fear was a characteristic of the life of the early Church. It was a fear which did not banish joy, peace and love. Rather it made these joy, peace and love in *God*— the *true* God—not in oneself nor in one's home-made God. The women ran from the empty tomb 'with fear and great joy.'[7] The churches in Judaea and Galilee and Samaria walked 'in the fear of the Lord and in the comfort of the Holy Ghost.'[8] The man in whom the Lord Christ dwells knows the joy which goes deep down into the heart of the

[1] Psa. 139: 9, 10.　[2] Heb. 10: 31.　[3] Heb. 12: 21; Ex. 19: 16 ff.
[4] Mat. 7: 6.　[5] Lu. 24: 37.　[6] Phil. 2: 12, A.R.S.V.　[7] Mat. 28: 8.
[8] Acts 9: 31.

holy God. His joy has substance and content *because* it is charged with fear. The fear of *God*.

To the extent that I stand in awe of God, I also stand in awe of myself. For the God whom I fear has made His home with me. He has made me one substance with Himself.[1] Shall I not be afraid? For it is *God* who has laid hold upon me. It is *He* who has united me with Himself.

Moreover, this is no static union. It is a living, progressive, developing union. It is a union which involves dynamic relation. A relation in which God, although dwelling in the person of the believer, yet continually breaks through into his life from beyond. Breaks through at this moment. And who knows in what fashion He will break through in the coming moment? Who knows what new form of the divine life He will fashion in the believer before to-day's sun sets?

We speak of a 'new form of the divine life' in the believer, for this is precisely what we mean when we say we 'are the Body of Christ and members in particular.'[2] This means that a new form of God's life walks the world in the person of every Christian. No wonder that he stands in awe of himself!

It is the fact that it is a *new* form of God's life which heightens his sense of awe beyond measure. The fact that the same Christ dwells in every Christian does not mean that each believer is a replica of every other believer. He is a *new* creation. He is not a stereotype. Certainly he shares in a nature which is common to all Christians; his whole being is transformed by God, but it is *his* whole being. And his participation in the being of

[1] cf. Calvin, *Institutes*, 4.17.3 and 11.   [2] 1 Cor, 12 : 27.

Christ is of such a sort as has never been before. This gives him such humility before God and such a reverence for his own person that he is able to avoid the ugly trap which opens up before him. He refuses to force his life into a ready-made mould. His actions are determined by the uniqueness of *his* new-found humanity. He copies no one. He does not even copy Christ. Despite Thomas à Kempis, he does not imitate his Lord. The apostle's affirmation, " I live, yet not I, but Christ liveth in me," [1] did not imply the substitution of Paul's personality by the personality of Jesus. Paul's personality was baptised into Christ, transformed by Christ —but it remained *Paul's* personality. God wanted *Paul*, not a puppet.

There is a profound sense in which God says to the believer, not " Be like Christ," but " Be yourself ! " Be, that is to say, the real, free, truly human self which God made you to be. It is in response to this gracious invitation that a man becomes the unique person God has ever intended him to be. He becomes himself. *Truly* himself. His whole being bears the stamp of originality and genuineness. It is the stamp of the God whose delight in creation is never exhausted. Now he is really free to be himself ; to act with a spontaneity, a poise, a holy confidence which spring from the nature which has been given to him and which has become his, really *his*.

And whilst he rejoices in his new being, he also stands in awe of it. He regards it with reverence and wonder. For whilst it is *his* freedom, *his* being, he knows that, at the same time, it is the freedom, it is the being of Almighty God. Where will this being lead him ? What will he, with his holy freedom, his own holy freedom, determine to do ? " Greater works than these shall he do." [2] He

[1] Gal. 2 : 20.   [2] Jn. 14 : 12.

reverences himself. And in this reverence there is fear as well as joy.

Likewise I bow in humble reverence before another in whom Christ dwells. He is a member of Christ's Body. He is one flesh with his Saviour. As I enter into relation with him, I also enter into relation with Christ.[1] I therefore approach him expectantly, eagerly. Who knows what the fruits of this encounter will be? The fine line drawn between time and eternity thins almost to breaking point when I meet my brother. I meet him *completely*. I meet him with my whole being. Likewise, he meets me. And, in this meeting, I am united to Christ. Through *him*! Will I not, therefore, reverence him through whom, and in whom, I enter into relation with God? I will not only reverence him; I will fear him with the holy fear which I have for God Himself. How could it be otherwise, when God dwells in him? I will fear him. And I will love him, too.

Each fresh meeting with this other will be an occasion for rejoicing and wonder. For God is always seeking to manifest Himself in new ways, His purpose is ever moving on and ever seeking expression in flesh and blood, especially where two or three are gathered together in the Name of Christ. And each introduction to another member of the Body must bring intense delight, joy, hope, awe. For here is another form of God's life abroad in the world! A form of God's life whose meeting with me is touched with such undercurrents of eternal reality that, for a moment, the veil is drawn aside, and I catch a glimpse of that holy love which ever lives between the Father and the Son and the Holy Spirit. I see, no doubt, ' in a glass darkly.' But I *see*!

Now, Christ comes to us through *all* men. For He is

[1] Eph. 5 : 21, A.R.S.V.

the Saviour of all men. To be sure, He is 'especially' the Saviour of those who believe in Him.[1] And that 'especially' makes an incalculable difference. And yet He is the Saviour of *all*, for He died for all, and He rose for all. This means that He has relation with all [2] even though all do not enjoy relation with Him. He is not only above all and through all, He is also *in* all (καὶ ἐν πᾶσιν).[2] He therefore approaches the believer in all whom he meets.

Hence the believer approaches the unbeliever with no less reverence and fear than when he approaches another believer. The one who comes to him is unable to enter into relation. But the believer enters into relation with *him*. For this relation is given by the Christ who is in all. Such an occasion may be revelation for the unbeliever. In however broken and fragmentary a fashion he will know himself to be in touch with a reality of a new dimension. With Kahlil Gibran he may well say—

> *Sweeter still than laughter*
> *And greater than longing came to me.*
> *It was the boundless in you ;* [3]

He knows not that 'the boundless' is the Christ.

For the believer this occasion will be charged with divine significance. Although his brother is not 'in Christ,' yet Christ is in his brother. Therefore, with what tenderness he meets him ! With what awe he approaches him ! He takes his brother seriously. He gives himself whole-heartedly to him. His brother is Thou and fills the heavens. He will not dare to put his brother 'in his place,' to gain ascendancy over him and thus do violence to him.[4] He remembers the words of the Mediator, " Inasmuch as ye have done it unto one of the least of these my brethren,

---

[1] 1 Tim. 4 : 10 ; cf. 1 Jn. 4 : 14 ; 2 Cor. 5 : 19.   [2] Eph. 4 : 6 ; cf. Ro. 11 : 29 ff.
[3] *The Prophet*, Heinemann, 1953, p. 81 f.   [4] cf. Dietrich Bonhoeffer, *Life Together*, Harper, 1954, p. 34 ff.

ye have done it unto Me." [1] Therefore, with wonder and gravity, he reverences his brother. [2]

Now, the man in whom the Lord Christ dwells is able to live the life of God. Not only does he cry, with Simone Weil, " Christ is present with me in person ! " [3] He also affirms, with Kagawa, " God is with*in* me ! " [4] Because of this he is amongst those who have discovered God's secret ' which has been hid from ages and from generations, but now is made manifest to his saints.' [5] The secret is simply this— " Christ in you ! " [6]

In the light of this secret, the astonishing demands which Christ makes of us take on a new meaning. We realise that He is *serious*. For He is demanding that we do nothing which He Himself did not do and nothing which He is not eager to do *in* us. We do not attempt to explain away the " Be ye therefore perfect, even as your Father which is in heaven is perfect," [7] but we realise that this is just as realistic a command as " Thou shalt love the Lord thy God with *all* thy heart, and with *all* thy soul, and with *all* thy mind." [8]

He who takes these demands seriously is, at first, overwhelmed by their absolute character and by the ' impossibility ' of obedience. But then he reflects upon the nature of the One who makes the demands. He remembers, as Quell and Stauffer assert, [9] that He was no mere utopian. ' He speaks of these impossible claims in tones of consistent earnestness and realism, as meaning what everybody can and should do. There have always been visionaries, dreaming of universal love and a better world. Jesus knows the world as it is, and yet calls on men to live the life of

---

[1] Mat. 25 : 40.   [2] cf. John Woolman's *Journal*, World Publishing Company, 1954, p. 64.   [3] *Waiting on God*, Routledge & Kegan Paul, 1952, p. 24.   [4] *op. cit.*, p. 15.   [5] Col. 1 : 26.   [6] Col. 1 : 27.   [7] Mat. 5 : 48 ; cf. Heb. 7 : 25. [8] Mat. 22 : 37 ; cf. Jn. 13 : 34.   [9] *Love*, A. & C. Black, tr. J. R. Coates, 1949, p. 49.

perfect love in this world. He does it in sober, objective seriousness.' This, as the writers go on to insist, implies one thing and one thing only. ' Jesus has more to proclaim than a new demand. He proclaims, He creates, a new world-situation.'

This ' new world-situation ' is what Paul calls ' a new creation.' It is a wholly new order of life. It is a new race of men. Men in whom God dwells. And because God dwells in them, they are *able* to live God's life. ' Christ has . . . now, through the Gospel, opened to us men the shining possibilities of the life that is eternal.'[1] *Now !* The gift of God *is* in us ![2]

The believer who knows that this is true is not concerned to argue the theoretical problem of Perfectionism. He has been called to obedience and to love. He therefore loves his God with all his heart and soul and mind, and he also loves his neighbour as himself.[3] His first concern is not to argue but to live and to be faithful—to meet the supernatural grace of God with a total response of faith. In that moment, when grace meets faith, the sinner knows that God is able to do more about sin than forgive it. He knows in actual experience that his defects are no hindrance to God's grace (' He has regarded the *lowliness* of His handmaid.') He knows, in terms which are intensely personal, what Christ meant when He said, " Ye shall receive power, after that the Holy Ghost is come upon you."[4] He knows that, by God's grace, he is *able* to live God's life.

Such a man has found himself. Or, rather, he has been found of God. No longer does he anxiously seek fulfilment. He has *found* fulfilment in the immediate presence of God. The present moment contains all he could wish

[1] 2 Tim. 1: 10. Phillip's translation. [2] 2 Tim. 1: 6. [3] Lu. 10: 27.
[4] Acts 1: 8.

for and much more besides. ' He is no longer anxious lest the future never yield all he has hoped, lest he fail to contribute his full stint before he passes on—he stands erect in the holy Now, serene, assured, unafraid. Instead of being the active, hurrying church worker and the anxious, careful planner of shrewd moves toward the good life, he becomes a pliant creature, less brittle, less obstinately rational.' [1] Upon him the ends of the world have come. He carries about within him that end for which God fashioned the universe—Jesus Christ his Lord.

When this happens to a man, something occurs which is decisive for human history. A miracle takes place. God is on the march in the world in a peculiar way. The Lord of all creation is at work in union with the believer. That work may escape even passing notice by the world. But the effect of that work, of that life, of that union, will echo down through eternity.

Thus far, we have been emphasising the fact of the believer's union with Christ. But there is a more fundamental fact which has made this union possible.

Throughout this study we have been insisting on the two-fold nature of the Church—as the real Body of Christ and as subject to Christ's Lordship. Nowhere is the significance of this double nature made more plain than in the life of the believer. He has been made one with his Lord ; he shares realistically in the divine-humanity of his Saviour. But he is profoundly conscious of the fact that this is not a state which he has himself brought about. The miracle is not understandable in terms of itself. The fact that he shares in Christ's divine-humanity cannot be explained in *terms* of Christ's divine-humanity. It can only be explained in terms of Christ's Lordship.

[1] Thomas Kelly, *op. cit.*, p. 74 f.

The believer who shares in the life of the Body of Christ, does so because that life has been *received* from Christ the Lord. He does so because it is a life which is being *continually* received from Christ the Lord. Christ is the sole source of his new humanity. Union with God, in all its parts, is the work and the gift of the exalted Lord.

Indeed, if this were not so, he would be profoundly disturbed. More, he would be alarmed, even terrified. To think that God, the living, the Almighty God, the Lord God Omnipotent dwells in *him*! If this were the whole truth would he not go mad? What explosive potential slumbers in his poor, frail being! What revolutionary forces may at any moment be unleashed in him! Let us make no mistake—the explosive potential and the revolutionary forces are undoubtedly present within him. But they belong to *Christ*. For *He* is the Lord!

When a man becomes aware of the fact that he not only lives *in* Christ's Body but that he also lives *under* Christ's Lordship, His loving, strengthening, forgiving Lordship, —then he is strong because he is weak; he is pure because he is freely forgiven; he has all things because he has nothing, nothing except Christ his Lord.

Union with God, therefore, has its birth in an awareness of Christ's Lordship. It does not begin when the believer seeks union with God. He may desire ' union-with-God ' more than he desires union with *God*. He may be straining after a *feeling* of union with a God of his own devising. He may be avoiding that God to whom one day he may well cry, " Why hast Thou forsaken me? " (although, to be sure, he will preface that cry with the great confession of faith, " My *God*, *my* God!)." No, union with God begins when a man becomes aware of the fact that Jesus Christ is *Lord*. And that is another way of saying that he becomes

aware of the fact that God is *God*—really *God*. It begins
with belief in God. ' Him that cometh unto God must
believe that He is.' [1] This is not as superficial an observation
as it may appear to be. We know that it is possible for the
' believer ' to have an exalted belief in doctrines *about* God
and no living belief in God Himself. His faith may have
its roots in his own *ideas* of God. Or it may have its source
in his admiration for the marvellous *works* of God. But
the time comes when, with Augustine, he is filled with a
profound dissatisfaction with the works of God—' beautiful
works of Thine, but *works* of Thine all the same and not
Thyself.' [2] And when he is brought to this state in which
he seriously desires God—God as the Awful, Holy, Loving,
Compassionate *Lord* of life—when, with George Fox, he
begins his ' passionate quest for the real whole-wheat Bread
of Life,' [3] he discovers that, when he hungers for bread he
does not receive a stone. And he remembers the word of
his Lord, " Him that cometh unto *Me*, I will in no wise
cast out." [4]

Union with God begins, we say, in that man who is
humble enough to believe in Christ as Lord. And he who
knows that Christ is Lord knows also that He is absolute
Lord or He is not Lord at all. He is the Lord who does
not want men's *deeds* but who wants *men*. Hence, belief in
this Lord—if it be serious, open-eyed belief—will inevitably
involve a complete detachment from all things, even holy
things, in order to cleave to the Lord Himself in all His
naked majesty and love. It will issue in what Brother
Lawrence called ' one hearty renunciation of everything
which we are sensible does not lead to God ' ; [5] a self-
renunciation which alone brings God-possession. And this
renunciation will have implications in every area of his

---

[1] Heb. 11 : 6.   [2] *Confessions*, Sheed & Ward, 1951, p. 35.   [3] Thomas Kelly,
op. cit., p. 45.   [4] Jn. 6 : 37.   [5] *Practice of the Presence of God*, Epworth Press,
p. 16.

life. It will mean a complete break with the standards and pre-suppositions of the world about him. It will involve a massive re-orientation of his total attitude to the world.

Now, without a profound awareness of the Lordship of Christ, such a renunciation will be impossible. If he does not believe that Christ is Lord—the *living* Lord—he will not trust Him with his life. He will be obliged to make his *own* plans for the future, and he will try to bring them about by his own little human means. He will *speak*, perchance, of ' abandonment to God,' but as soon as God begins to dispose of him according to His infinite wisdom, he will protest and draw back and it will be seen that his ' abandon ' was only a meaningless word.[1] It was not abandon to *God* . . . But, let us repeat, such abandon is impossible, quite impossible, if he does not seriously *believe* in God—if he does not believe that Christ is *Lord*. Without such belief, he will follow Christ in principle, but he will not follow Him in practice. ' There are plenty to follow our Lord half-way,' wrote Meister Eckhart, ' but not the other half. They will give up possessions, friends and honours, *but it touches them too closely to disown themselves.*'[2] And yet, when the truth is borne in upon them that the Christ who confronts them is the Lord of all creation, the Lord from whom, at the beginning, they have come, the Lord to whom, at the end, they will return, the Lord upon whom, every moment of their days, they constantly depend—*then* the great renunciation comes. But not till then.

Only then are men able to understand that the Christian life is all contained in the confession—" Jesus is Lord."

---

[1] cf Dom Marmion, *op. cit.*, p. 155.   [2] Quoted by Thomas Kelly, *op. cit.*, p. 43 f.

Only then are men able to live without any plan or project, save the project of belonging entirely to God.

If union with God is born in an awareness of the Lordship of Christ, it grows deeper by the same means. Just as the Church as a whole becomes more and more what she already is in her essence by a deepening awareness of the majesty, the presentness and the infinite love of her Lord, so with the believer. Hence, participation in the divine nature becomes a conscious and a manifest reality in direct proportion to the believer's faith in Christ as Lord. Many things are involved in deepening and sharpening his faith in Christ's Lordship. Some have already been discussed. We shall mention three more.

"Come ye yourselves apart into a desert place," said Jesus to His disciples. 'And they departed into a desert place by ship privately.'[1] 'And when He had sent (the multitudes) away, He departed into a mountain to pray.'[2]

If the believer is to be a follower of *Christ*, it is certain that he must spend most of his life in that world which clamours beyond the quiet of the sanctuary. We may say, however, with equal force, that if he is to be a follower of Christ, he must also turn his back upon that world, however costly and painful that 'turning' may be. If his life is to be conditioned, not by the world, but by God and the Gospel, he must 'send the multitudes away.'

There are those who deny the need for such 'withdrawal,' and who quote a master of the spiritual life in their support. 'The time of business does not with me differ from the time of prayer; and in the noise and clatter of my

[1] Mk. 6: 31.   [2] Mk. 6: 46; cf. 7: 24; 9: 30; 14: 32; Mat. 14: 23; 17: 1 f.; Lu. 5: 16; 9: 10; 18: 28; 11: 1; 4: 42; 6: 12; cf. 10: 29-37, with vv. 38-42; Jn, 6: 15; 8: 1; 11: 54; 12: 36.

kitchen, while several persons are at the same time calling for different things, I possess God in as great tranquillity as if I were upon my knees at the Blessed Sacrament.' [1] But Brother Lawrence only reached this state after ten hard years of spiritual discipline ; [2] and, having reached this state, he *continued* to keep the set hours of prayer and was found daily upon his knees ' at the Blessed Sacrament.'

' It is as much our duty,' writes Frank Laubach, ' to live in the beauty of the presence of God on some mount of transfiguration until we become white with Christ, as it is for us to go down where they grope and grovel and groan, and lift them to new life.' [3]

There is but one purpose in withdrawal. That purpose is communion with God. It is such an unconditional exposure of the depths of one's being to God as brings immediate contact with Him. In this communion He imparts His life to the believer, penetrating the recesses of his heart and soul and mind, and making him, in all seriousness, partaker in His nature.

This communion takes place supremely in the Sacrament of the Lord's Supper. Here, in the feast, Christ offers Himself to the believer. Here, in response to the believer's " Come, Lord Jesus ! " Christ is formed in him. It is Christ *Himself* who is formed in him. With à Kempis he prays, " I seek not Thy gifts but *Thyself* ! " [4] and Christ does not fail to answer his prayer. He whose divine-humanity is the sole source of the believer's life, enters into the depths of his being and makes him a new creation.

In a manner inferior only to the celebration of the sacrament, the believer also finds communion with God in prayer and in the study of the Scriptures. Here all pretence is put aside as he seeks, not prayer nor the written Word, but the living Lord who comes to him in both.

[1] *op. cit.*, p. 23. [2] *op. cit.*, p. 29. [3] *op. cit.*, p. 35. [4] *op. cit.*, p. 241.

Without such communion with his Lord, he never rises above mediocrity in the life of faith, however busy and however active he may be. It is *in* such communion that God does more for his growth in grace than could be achieved by a lifetime of eloquent prayers or of unusual or uplifting thoughts. More is achieved in a single moment of direct contact with God than in a decade of abstract theological study.

Let it be emphasised that this communion will normally be given through the celebration of the Sacrament and through the discipline of that profound meditation which can grow out of prayer and Bible study. It is a communion which may or may not involve 'feelings.' But it *is* a communion in which we are found by the living God. A communion in which we pause, at peace, in His presence. It is a communion which lodges His Word, Himself, so deeply in our hearts that He holds and refreshes and fortifies us throughout the busy day. It is a communion which equips us for our life with Him in His world. It does so because He is the *Lord*.

" Watch ye, therefore," said Jesus, " and pray always." [1] And no doubt Paul had this injunction in mind when he urged the Christians at Ephesus to be ' praying always with all prayer and supplication in the Spirit and watching thereunto with all perseverance.' [2] And to the Church at Thessalonica, ' Pray without ceasing.' [3]

When the believer comes down from the Mount, he is still in the presence of his Lord. And his life is entirely dependent upon His presence. Being profoundly aware of this dependence, his thoughts often rise to the source of his life. In the midst of his many duties, his prayers are

[1] Lu. 21: 36.   [2] Eph. 6: 18.   [3] 1 Thes. 5: 17; cf. Ro. 12: 12; Lu. 18: 1; 11: 5-7. Col. 1: 39.

directed to this source. Working at his bench, or sitting at his desk, he finds himself engaging in familiar conversation with Him. An undercurrent of worship sustains his life in the world. All his activities, however trivial they may appear to be, are upheld and informed by the prayer which arises from and which is directed to the Christ who is both within him and above him, to the Mediator who is the Lord of his union with God.

It may be many years before he confesses with Brother Lawrence, " It is as difficult for me not to think of God as at first it was to do so."[1] He may never reach the stage at which he cries, " I believe no more, but I see ! "[2] Yet, if his awareness of the Lordship of Christ has made him conscious of the fact that He is *Lord of the Here and Now*, and if this consciousness has brought the response of a child-like communion with his ever-present Lord, he becomes ἄνθρωπος τέλειος,[3] a complete man, a man who has ' centred down ' in his Maker, a man beneath whose outward life surges the life of God.

' God was in Christ reconciling *the world* unto Himself.'[4] He was not only reconciling humanity—He was reconciling *the world*. All things are reconciled to God, in Christ. Not only all *men*, but all *things*. That is to say that behind the most common object and behind the most trivial toil, stands God. Back of the It dwells the Eternal Thou. And the Thou breaks through the It continually.

When one reflects seriously upon the significance of the Incarnation, one is bound to glimpse something of the vast and universal—as well as the minute and the particular—consequences which have followed this never-to-be-repeated event. It is the ' *whole creation* '[5] which has been

---

[1] *op. cit.*, p. 22.   [2] *ibid.*, p. 55.   [3] Mat. 5 : 48; Col. 1 : 28; cf. Ja. 1 : 8.
[4] 2 Cor. 5 : 19.   [5] Ro. 8 : 19-23.

grasped, as it were, in the hand of God, that ' He might gather together in one *all things* in Christ.' [1]

That is to say that Christ is the Lord of all things, He has relation to all things, He is to be found in all things.[2] Nothing is too common to escape this reconciliation. Nothing is so mean as to be denied relation with Him. In Christ, God has personal relation with every thing, and disposes every thing—literally every *thing*—for the good of the believer who discerns behind ' all things ' [3] the gracious approach of God.

It is for this reason that the believer accepts every situation as God's layout for that hour. He does not take his own importance or his own schedule too seriously. He allows his programme to be interrupted by God. He does not refuse the unexpected menial task, lest he refuse his Lord. Indeed, he will welcome a life which is given over to such tasks. Behind the most lowly occupation, behind the most commonplace object, he perceives, with thankful wonder, the image of the Mediator. With the Emmaus disciples, he breaks through the bread and behold !—the Lord is here !

[1] Eph., 1 : 10.   [2] Eph., 4 : 6   [3] Ro. 8 : 28.

CONCLUSION

MISSION, Gospel, ethics and sanctification find their unity in Christ. They all consist in the life of Christ. They are all inspired by the Lordship of Christ. They are not separate aspects of life. They are *life*. They are a living whole.

And it is this organic ' wholeness ' of the Christian life, of the Church, which is the only hope for a world whose (frequently confused and unintentional) sin imprisons it in a massive, self-destructive, man-centred unity from which it is powerless to set itself free. This unity of the world can be broken and re-fashioned in the image of God only by the means through which the process of re-creation was begun—by the Creator of the universe at work in Jesus Christ.

Christ was confronted with a fundamentally united world which presented a solid front in hostile opposition to His mission. No mere man could break through that front. Christ broke through it because His manhood was united to the Godhead in such a way that mankind was exposed to nothing less than the powerful love of the Creator. Christ broke the unity of the world with the higher unity of the Trinity. His weapon was the life of God made manifest in His love, His obedience, His willingness to die. The world had no weapons in her armoury with which to match this weapon. She could not vanquish God.

As with Christ, so with His Body. The key to the Church's mission is not to be found in the realm of re-organisation : God seeks not a Church *galvanised* into action but a Church made *alive* by Him. Nor is it to be found firstly in the immensely hopeful revival in Biblical studies which is gathering momentum both in the Roman Catholic Church[1] and in the Protestant Church : " This Biblical theology," said Emil Brunner in 1952, " has been preached in Switzerland for nearly ten years with little apparent effect " ; Biblical theology, proclaimed by word of mouth alone, can become as much an idol as Israel's golden calf. The key is not even to be found only in love—a love which goes forth in word and deed and sacrifices itself for the world : ' love ' may be nothing more than sentiment ; it may be as superficial and vain as it is costly and painful. The key to the Church's mission is to be found in the person of Christ alone. The Church penetrates the solid front of the world and re-fashions it in the likeness of God, not firstly by techniques or theology or love, but by nothing less than God in Christ, by her manhood united to the Godhead, by the life of God in the life of His people whom He sends into the world as He sent His Son into the world.

Here we are concerned not with ' abstract theology ' but with ultimate reality, with God Himself in Christ. We are free to seek reality elsewhere. We are at liberty to join the company of those who go forward trusting only in ' the guidance of the Spirit.' But let us be quite clear concerning the nature of this ' Spirit ' in whose company we undertake our pilgrimage. Is it the *Holy* Spirit ? Or is it the spirit of man, striving to re-make the world after his own confused image ? Or is it, perchance, some other

[1] cf. the work of Père la Grange, O.S.D., which is reflected in such widely used publications as ' *Initiation de l'enfant au Mystere Chrétien par la Bible et la Liturgie*,' Editions Fleurus, Paris, 1952. See especially pp. 49-50—' Il est nécessaire que chaque enfant possède une Histoire Sainte et un Evangile. Les textes peuvent être utilisés indépendamment de l'enseignement catéchistique lui-même.'

spirit, some strange, unlovely spirit, guiding us down some arduous, noble by-way which leads neither us, nor others for whom Christ lives, unto the city of God? Or *is* it the Holy Spirit? The One who speaks in unmistakable terms of Jesus Christ [1] and who leads men into all Truth? This is the only Spirit who leads the Church into the way of reality, of unity, of incarnation, of crucifixion, of resurrection, of Christ. And this is the way which the Church must walk if she is to be faithful to her Lord.

But our main concern in this study has been to show, not so much that the Church *must* follow this way of Christ, but that the Church is *able* to follow this way. The Church has almost always known what she *ought* to do; only rarely has this knowledge been translated into action. She has known full well what she ought to do and she has been incapable of doing it. But once the Church knows not only what she *ought*, but also what she *is*—what she is in her innermost being—*then* she will be *able* to follow her Lord. For the Church lives by faith. By grace Christ has made her one Body with Himself. By faith she may become in fact what she already is in her essence.

So long as the Church believes that her human nature has not been radically transformed, her nature will *remain* human nature. But when the Church believes that the very life of the risen Christ has become *her* life, in fact and not in fantasy; when the Church gathers around her Lord's Table and believes that she receives, not hollow symbols of Christ, but Christ Himself with all His benefits; when the Church believes that the same divine-humanity which rose triumphant from the grave has become *her* humanity, the substance of her being and the organic source of her life— *then* the Church will be *able* to pursue the goal which her Lord has set before her, and God Himself will be abroad

[1] Jn. 14: 26; 15: 26; 16: 13, 14.

in the world no less than when He walked in Galilee. And then His life will be made manifest not in Galilee only, but wherever this Church, His Body on earth, knows that she is in fact His Body, living thankfully under His Lordship and, therefore, living by the power which raised Him from the dead.

So far as her own life and action is concerned, the Church knows but one ultimately creative force in history. That force is to be found where grace meets faith. In the providence of God, grace is not enough. He respects our human will. Faith must answer grace.

Grace came down upon a virgin in Nazareth. It was answered by her faithful cry, " Be it unto me in accordance with Thy will." In the marriage of grace and faith, Jesus Christ was conceived and born into the world. Here was One who was full of grace. But only by the human response of His faith to the movement of divine grace was the New Humanity, the Church, conceived and born into the world. In His life, His death, His resurrection, all that was needful for the free activity of the powerful grace of God in His Church has been done. There is no reason on *God's* side why His Church should not express precisely the same miraculous, transforming life as was expressed in the person of His Son.

All that is needful is faith.

INDEX OF NAMES

Aaron, 22
Abraham, 63, 144
Allen, Roland, 146
Allshorn, Florence, 137
Athanasius, 149
Augustine, 172

Barth, Karl, 20, 41, 124, 133
Bonhoeffer, D., 36, 90, 130, 138f
Bruce, Robert, 40, 66
Brunner, Emil, 180
Buber, Martin, 75, 152
Buddha, Gautama, 66

Calvin, John, 35, 39, 135, 155
Camfield, F. W., 129
Cullmann, O., 36, 58, 66

Daniel, 24f
David, 145
Davidson, A. B., 124
Dostoievsky, 98

Eckhart, 173
Eliot, T. S., 109
Ellul, Jacques, 105, 153f
Ezekiel, 24, 86

Fox, George, 153, 172
Francis of Assisi, 156
Fry, Christopher, 148

Gibran, Kahlil, 167

Hendry, G. S., 72
Hitler, Adolf, 107, 142
Hunter, A. M., 48

Isaiah, 15, 26f, 118

John Baptist, 106
John, St., 23, 26, 29, 63, 68, 71, 120, 126, 140
Josephus, 56

Kagawa, 97, 161, 168
Kelly, Thomas, 99, 151, 161, 170
Kempis, Thomas à, 155, 165, 175
Kierkegaard, S., 19, 98
Kraemar, Hendrik, 140

Laubach, F., 155, 175
Lawrence, Brother, 172, 175, 177
Lazarus, 107, 160
Lehmann, Paul L., 103, 128, 139
Loew, Father, 97
Luther, Martin, 35, 39, 134f, 144, 151

Mackintosh, H. R., 107, 114
Macleod, George, 15
Manson, William, 29
Marmion, Dom Columba, 151, 173
Mary, 69, 72, 104, 182
Michonneau, Abbé, 89, 97, 100f
Morton, T. Ralph, 106
Moses, 14, 100, 145, 163

Niebuhr, Reinhold, 131
Nietzsche, 102

Paul, St., 31, 33, 44, 62, 68, 71, 73, 120, 126, 140, 146, 150
Peter, St., 20, 46, 61, 71, 73, 76, 120, 126, 140
Philip, 62
Pliny, 56

Quell and Stauffer, 159, 168

Ramsey, A. M., 19
Rieu, E. V., 124
Robinson, J. A. T., 20, 33
Rupp, Gordon, 109, 134, 135

Schmidt, Hans, 124
Schmidt, K. L., 35, 48
Scougal, Henry, 151
Shaw, G. B., 130
Smith, George Adam, 109
Stephen, St., 29, 34
Stewart, J. S., 60, 140, 151

Temple, William, 103
Thomas, St., 90
Torrance, T. F., 42, 135

Warren, M. A. C., 96
Weil, Simone, 168
Wesley, John, 41
Woolman, John, 168

INDEX OF SUBJECTS

Acceptance, 98, 133, 155–62

Action and being, 14f, 152f, 158, 181

Adultery, 145

Anarchy, 146

Assassination, 142

Atonement, 15, 23, 84, 98, 115–21, 133

Augsburg Confession, 87

Authority, 101

Awakening, spiritual, 114, 121, 123, 154–8

Awe of God, 162–4; of self, 164–6; of neighbour, 166–8

Baptism, 23, 26, 69, 72, 85, 86, 88, 116, 118, 124–6

Barmen Declaration, 107

Body of Christ, 27f, 31–42, 71f, 88, 95, 127, 133–6, 146, 149, 166, 182

Body, Head of, 43–65, 78, 127

Bride, 31

Buddhist, spirituality, 66; anthropology, 75

Building, 31

Christ, ascended, 30, 45, 63, 104; as Creator, 63f; conception of, 69, 182; divinity of, 47–65, 128; forgives sin, 51; humanity of, 20, 68, 70; identical with Church, 16, 25, 35f; as Judge, 44; lordship of, 68, 78, 140, 170–8; mission of, 84f; present activity of, 147; real presence of, 100, 139, 168; rule of, 61–4; second coming of, 45f; sinful flesh of, 19, 20, 23; sinlessness of, 21; teaching of, 128, 141; temptations of, 21, 73; as ultimate reality, 132f, 136, 180; ultimate triumph of, 64; in the unbeliever, 167; union with, 15, 148, 152ff, 157, 162, 164, 166, 168, 170

Christian as creator, 144, 148, 158, 173; as victim, 97

Church and Christ identical, 35f; as Bride, 32; as Building, 31; as Body, 33–42; as Christ's patron, 43, 45; destiny of, 74, 77, 79; essential nature of, 13f, 73, 181; predicament

of, 14; sin of, 44; sufferings of, 85–90, 106; triumph of, 100f, 181f

Circumcision, 84

Corinth, church at, 67f, 146

Confidence, 100, 156, 170

Community, 96

Conversion, 61, 73, 93, 95, 105, 151, 154, 172f

Covenant, 27, 39, 52, 84, 118

Cross, 28, 87, 92, 99, 115, 133–5; and forgiveness, 115–21; necessity of, 117; uniqueness of, 119

Cup of suffering, 26f, 86, 118

Decalogue, 84, 129, 132, 141f, 144

Disciples, dependence on Christ, 64; dependence on Church, 95; doubts of, 56; failure of, 112; miracles of, 61, 73; mission of, 85; power of, 61; and risen Christ, 70f

Doubt, necessity of, 47

Easter, 56f, 71, 99, 128

Economic law, 103

Ends and means, 155

Ethical insecurity, 146

Ethics, 128–48

Eucharist, 27f, 36–42, 52, 58, 67, 94, 147, 175f, 181

Exodus, the, 84, 103, 141

Faith, 46f, 93, 169, 172f, 181f; irrelevance of, 129; lack of, 14f, 37f, 57

Fall, the, 138

Fear, loss of, 157f, 161, 170; of God, 162–4

Following Christ, 110–13, 115, 168, 181

Forgiveness, 95f, 111, 113–21, 125, 133–6, 143, 145, 147, 157–9

Fornication, 67, 146

Forty days, the, 54, 56, 70

Freedom, 77, 120, 135, 146, 147, 153, 156, 158, 165

Friday, Good, 99, 128

Galatians, 150

God, alone with, 147, 156; a man before, 148; as Creator, 143; as Father,

76f, 86 ; as Lawgiver, 141 ; being of, 124, 151 ; communion with, 159, 175 ; fear of, 162–4 ; image of, 91, 179 ; initiative of, 76, 93, 114, 141, 147, 154, 169, 176 ; in man's image, 129, 162f, 171, 180 ; love of, 159–64 ; real presence of, 154, 160, 163, 168f ; will of, 110, 137–48
Gospel, 103–27
Greek spirituality, 66, 74
Guilt, 114, 120

Healing, 61
Hebrews, 120, 126
Hindu spirituality, 66f
History, 29, 53, 63, 131, 141, 147, 153, 170, 182
Holiness, 101
Hymns, 59

Identification, Christ with Christian, 35, 149ff ; Christ with Church, 25, 26, 27, 28, 33, 34, 36, 37, 38–42, 71, 85f ; Christ with humanity, 22, 23, 29, 84f ; Christian with Church, 94–6 ; Church with Christ, 91–4 ; Church with humanity, 86f, 96–102
Idolatry, 43, 47, 144, 146
Immortality, 40
Incarnation, 19–30, 67f, 84, 86f, 104, 133 ; extension of, 43
Indian mysticism, 74
Individual, 152
Israel, 14, 22, 46, 103f, 144

Jerusalem Conference, 109
Jerusalem Council, 146
Judgment, 135
Justification, 134 ; self-, 134

Kingdom of God, 64, 69, 96, 146, 154f
Knowledge of good and evil, 138

Law, 104, 128–32, 141f, 145 ; transcended, 143, 145f
Life, unified, 140
Little Sisters of Jesus, 101
Logic, frailty of, 53
Love, 105, 107, 157, 159–63, 166, 169

Macedonia, 62
Man, 'established,' 153 ; estrangement of, 131 ; loneliness of, 152 ; 'ideal,'

156 ; 'religious,' 131, 152; weakness of, 111
Martyrdom, 87, 118
Material, Christian conception of, 69–72, 84, 177f
'Materialistic' Christianity, 103–8
Maturity, 147f, 153, 170
Mediator, 92, 101, 152, 177f
Meeting, 75, 152, 159, 166–8
Messiah, 24
Mission, 84–102, 127, 180
Morality, 147
Moslem, 75

Name, the, 124
Now, the, 160, 169, 170, 177

Obedience, 168f

Peace, 158, 170
Pentecost, 45
Perfectionism, 169
Person, 74–8, 109, 151f, 157 ; unique, 165
Personal relation, 75–8, 109f, 130, 137, 143, 152f
Personal responsibility, 146
Personality, unified, 152
Pharisee, 138f, 144f
Philosophy, 129
Politics, 103, 109
Power, 61, 72–4, 90, 168–70
Prayer, 27, 58, 65, 174–7
Priest, 22, 101
Priest-workers, 94
Principles, 111, 129ff, 146
Prodigal son, 145
Purpose of God, 109f, 127, 136, 138, 143, 147, 151, 166, 170, 181 ; fulfilled in Christ, 133 ; fulfilled in Christian, 148

Reconciliation, 133, 139, 147 ; of world, 178
Reformers, 35, 37
Relation, 152, 158f, 161, 167
Repentance, 116, 145
Resurrection, 54–9, 69, 70, 87, 122, 125, 133 ; and crucifixion, 88. 100 ; evidence for, 55–9
Revelation, 129, 140
Roman Empire, 15, 63, 126
Rome, 62, 106

Sabbath, 145
Scripture, 175f
Servant, Suffering, 24, 26, 119
Sin, 138, 157, 169, 179
Social concern, 67, 103–8
Son of God, 26, 49ff, 72
Son of man, 23–6, 29, 32
Spirit, Holy, 53, 59f, 68–79, 122, 180
Spiritual Body, 66–79 ; physical nature of, 68–72 ; power of, 72–4 ; personal nature of, 74–8
' Spiritual,' irrelevance of the, 66
Spirituality, a false, 38, 67, 107
Substitution, 119
Suffering, power of, 90
Sufferings of Christ, 26, 34, 84–7 ; of Church, 85–90, 106
Suicide, 142
Sunday, 57

Temple, *vide* Building
Theology, 83, 149, 154
Tongues, 67
Transubstantiation, 37
Trinity, 35, 84, 109, 179

Union with God, 15, 74, 96, 121–7, 148, 160, 164, 166, 171, 175

Vine and branches, 32, 38, 123, 149f
Virgins, wise, 146

Withdrawal, necessity of, 174–6
Word of God, 94f
World, a questioning, 91, 129 ; a reconciled, 177 ; of make-believe, 157
World Council of Churches, 48
Worship, 59, 155, 177

Yahweh, 143

INDEX OF BIBLICAL REFERENCES

GENESIS
1.28 : *p.* 103
2.7 : *p.* 77
3.5 : *p.* 92
4.1 : *p.* 159
22.2 : *p.* 144
22.10 : *p.* 100
28.17 : *p.* 44
32.24ff : *p.* 89

EXODUS
3.6 : *p.* 44
3.12 : *p.* 14
16.20 : *p.* 46
19.16ff : *p.* 100, 163
28.12 : *p.* 22, 101
28.29 : *p.* 101
28.30 : *p.* 22
28.36 : *p.* 101

LEVITICUS
20.10 : *p.* 145
24.16 : *p.* 51
25.10ff : *p.* 104

DEUTERONOMY
5.6 : *p.* 103
6.12 : *p.* 103

JOSHUA
3.17 : *p.* 88
11.6, 14f : *p.* 144

I SAMUEL
10.6 : *p.* 69

JOB
28.28 : *p.* 162

PSALMS
2.7 : *p.* 26, 72
139.7 : *p.* 160
139.9, 10 : *p.* 163

ISAIAH
5.13 : *p.* 15
6.5 : *p.* 44, 162
40.23, 25 : *p.* 162

42.1 : *p.* 26
42.1–4 : *p.* 85
44.17, 20 : *p.* 162
51.17 : *p.* 27
53. : *p.* 118
53.10 : *p.* 86, 26
57.15 : *p.* 162
58.6f : *p.* 104
60.1–22 : *p.* 103
65.25 : *p.* 103

JEREMIAH
2.5 : *p.* 109
20.9 : *p.* 155
23.23 : *p.* 162
31.31 : *p.* 52

EZEKIEL
3.15 : *p.* 24, 87
9.4 : *p.* 87
37.1–14 : *p.* 77

DANIEL
3.25 : *p.* 100
7.13, 14, 18 : *p.* 25

AMOS
5.12, 16, 21f : *p.* 104
9.11–15 : *p.* 103

HABAKKUK
2.14 : *p.* 103

ZECHARIAH
12.2 : *p.* 27
14.9 : *p.* 103

MALACHI
1.11 : *p.* 103

MATTHEW
1.20 : *p.* 69
1.23 : *p.* 86
2.14 : *p.* 104
3.16 : *p.* 69
4.1 : *p.* 69
4.18, 22 : *p.* 110
5.7–9 : *p.* 110

5.11 : *p.* 110
5.18 : *p.* 144
5.22, 28, 34, 39, 44 : *p.* 146
5.42 : *p.* 146
5.44f : *p.* 110
5.48 : *p.* 168, 177
6.12–15 : *p.* 111
7.21 : *p.* 137
7.21–27 : *p.* 110
7.22 : *p.* 106
8.19 : *p.* 110
8.22 : *p.* 110
8.29 : *p.* 156
9.2 : *p.* 111
9.9 : *p.* 110
9.13 : *p.* 116, 157
10.22 : *p.* 108, 110
10.22f : *p.* 108
10.35, 37 : *p.* 145
10.40 : *p.* 53, 150
11.3 : *p.* 49
11.20ff : *p.* 108
11.25ff : *p.* 49
11.27 : *p.* 102
12.6, 8 : *p.* 145
12.28 : *p.* 48
12.31 : *p.* 111
12.38ff : *p.* 117
13.33 : *p.* 123
14.23 : *p.* 174
14.30 : *p.* 112
14.33 : *p.* 54
15.4ff : *p.* 145
16.16 : *p.* 54
16.19 : *p.* 116
16.21 : *p.* 85, 117
16.23 : *p.* 112
16.24 : *p.* 86
16.25 : *p.* 110
16.27 : *p.* 25
17.1f : *p.* 174
17.5 : *p.* 51, 156
17.6 : *p.* 44, 163
17.14–18 : *p.* 105
17.16ff : *p.* 61, 112
18.15–22 : *p.* 116
18.21 : *p.* 111
19.8ff : *p.* 146

19.21, 28 : *p.* 110
21.28f : *p.* 116
21.29–31 : *p.* 110
21.33ff : *p.* 117
22.37 : *p.* 168
23.2ff : *p.* 146
23.33 : *p.* 137
24.9 : *p.* 86
24.13 : *p.* 110
24.30 : *p.* 25
25.1ff, 9 : *p.* 146
25.31 : *p.* 25
25.36, 43 : *p.* 105
25.40 : *p.* 34, 110, 168
25.41 : *p.* 106
26.2, 12 : *p.* 117
26.26 : *p.* 38
26.27 : *p.* 27
26.28 : *p.* 111, 118
26.31 : *p.* 117
26.35 : *p.* 112
26.39 : *p.* 21, 27, 118
26.52, 53 : *p.* 118
26.54 : *p.* 117
26.56 : *p.* 105, 117
26.65 : *p.* 51
27.43 : *p.* 50
27.51 : *p.* 104
28.1 : *p.* 58
28.4, 5, 8 : *p.* 162
28.6ff : *p.* 55
28.8 : *p.* 162, 163
28.9 : *p.* 54, 71
28.18 : *p.* 54, 64
28.18f : *p.* 73
28.19 : *p.* 116, 124
28.20 : *p.* 100

MARK
1.11 : *p.* 26, 51, 85, 156
1.13 : *p.* 51
1.15 : *p.* 116
1.24 : *p.* 156
2.5 : *p.* 51, 111
2.7 : *p.* 51, 52
3.5 : *p.* 137
3.28 : *p.* 111
3.35 : *p.* 137
4.12 : *p.* 111
6.2 : *p.* 72
6.7 : *p.* 95
6.12 : *p.* 116
6.31 : *p.* 174

6.46 : *p.* 174
6.56 : *p.* 105
7.18 : *p.* 112
7.24 : *p.* 174
8.22–6 : *p.* 105
8.31f : *p.* 117
8.34f : *p.* 110
9.12 : *p.* 117
9.30 : *p.* 174
9.31 : *p.* 117
10.29 : *p.* 111, 145
10.30 : *p.* 86, 111
10.32f : *p.* 117
10.34 : *p.* 26
10.38ff : *p.* 26
10.39 : *p.* 86
10.45 : *p.* 119
11.25 : *p.* 111
12.1–9 : *p.* 49
13.13 : *p.* 111
13.26 : *p.* 49
13.32, 34 : *p.* 49
13.34–7 : *p.* 110
14.22 : *p.* 27, 38, 87
14.24 : *p.* 27, 52
14.32 : *p.* 174
14.49 : *p.* 117
14.62 : *p.* 25, 49, 50
15.32 : *p.* 108
15.34 : *p.* 21, 118
15.39 : *p.* 89
16.2 : *p.* 58
16.9 : *p.* 58
16.11 : *p.* 56, 57
16.12 : *p.* 55
16.14 : *p.* 55
16.16 : *p.* 116
16.20 : *p.* 61

LUKE
1.1–4 : *p.* 59
1.26–38 : *p.* 51
1.35 : *p.* 69, 72
2.7 : *p.* 104
2.51 : *p.* 144
3.11 : *p.* 106
4.1–7 : 73
4.2 : *p.* 105
4.3, 9 : *p.* 108
4.13 : *p.* 21
4.14 : *p.* 72, 73
4.18 : *p.* 69, 72
4.32 : *p.* 72

4.42 : *p.* 174
5.8 : *p.* 44
5.12ff : *p.* 105
5.16 : *p.* 174
5.20 : *p.* 111
6.12 : *p.* 174
6.37 : *p.* 111
7.47–50 : *p.* 111
7.48f : *p.* 51
8.4ff : *p.* 123
9.10 : *p.* 174
9.23–5 : *p.* 111
9.31 : *p.* 86, 117
9.51 : *p.* 86, 117
10.1 : *p.* 95
10.17 : *p.* 112
10.27 : *p.* 169
10.29–37 : *p.* 174
10.38–42 : *p.* 174
11.1 : *p.* 174
11.4 : *p.* 111
11.5–7 : *p.* 176
11.20 : *p.* 48
12.10 : *p.* 111
12.50 : *p.* 26, 117, 118
13.33 : *p.* 117
15.7f, 10, 11–32 : *p.* 116
15.12, 29f : *p.* 145
16.30 : *p.* 116
16.31 : *p.* 59
17.3 : *p.* 111
17.25 : *p.* 117
18.1 : *p.* 176
18.13 : *p.* 43
18.22 : *p.* 110
18.28 : *p.* 174
19.9 : *p.* 110
21.36 : *p.* 176
22.15, 37 : *p.* 117
22.19 : *p.* 38
22.20 : *p.* 39
22.28f : *p.* 110
22.24, 50 : *p.* 112
22.29f : *p.* 38
22.37 : *p.* 117, 118
22.42 : *p.* 21
22.43 : *p.* 51
23.14–25 : *p.* 105
23.34 : *p.* 111, 133
24.11 : *p.* 57
24.13 : *p.* 58
24.13ff : *p.* 55
24.18 : *p.* 57

24.21 : p. 56
24.25–7 : p. 54
24.26, 46 : p. 117
24.30 : p. 55, 71
24.31 : p. 71
24.33, 36 : p. 58
24.34 : p. 55
24.36ff : p. 55
24.37 : p. 57, 163
24.37–9 : p. 70
24.41, 52 : p. 57
24.42f : p. 70
24.44ff : p. 54
24.46 : p. 117
24.47 : p. 111
24.52 : p. 57

JOHN
1.3 : p. 64
1.12 : p. 149
2.13–17 : p. 137
2.19–21 : p. 31
3.5–8 : p. 69
3.14 : p. 117
4.34 : p. 137
5.13 : p. 105
5.18 : p. 51
5.30 : p. 21, 137
6.15 : p. 174
6.37 : p. 172
6.38 : p. 137
6.51 : p. 117
6.53ff : p. 32
6.56 : p. 124
7.17 : p. 137
8.1 : p. 174
8.5 : p. 145
8.28 : p. 117
8.42, 58 : p. 63
9.35ff : p. 50
10.10 : p. 123
10.11ff : p. 117
10.28 : p. 136
10.30 : p. 53
10.33, 36 : p. 51
10.37f : p. 90
11.16 : p. 112
11.54 : p. 174
12.7, 23–7 : p. 118
12.24ff : p. 117
12.27 : p. 21
12.36 : p. 174
12.49 : p. 53

13.15 : p. 36
13.16 : p. 86
13.20 : p. 53
13.34 : p. 36, 168
14.6 : p. 102
14.7 : p. 53
14.12 : p. 36, 72, 165
14.16 : p. 76
14.26 : p. 181
15.1ff : p. 32
15.4 : p. 123
15.4f : p. 149
15.4ff : p. 30
15.20 : p. 86
15.26 : p. 76, 78, 181
16.13f : p. 76, 78, 181
16.28 : p. 63
17.11 : p. 124
17.18 : p. 86, 96
17.21ff : p. 124
17.22f, 26 : p. 150
17.23ff : p. 30
19.7 : p. 51
19.12, 23 : p. 105
19.27 : p. 144
19.28 : p. 105
20.15 : p. 57
20.19 : p. 57, 58, 71
20.19ff : p. 55
20.21 : p. 85
20.22 : p. 77
20.25 : p. 90
20.27 : p. 70
20.28 : p. 54, 90
20.31 : p. 124
21.9, 13, 15 : p. 71
21.12 : p. 56
21.18 : p. 100

ACTS
1.1 : p. 60
1.2f : p. 54
1.3 : p. 56, 71
1.8 : p. 72, 169
1.11 : p. 30
1.12 : p. 56
1.22 : p. 57, 122
2.14ff : p. 122
2.17–21, 33 : p. 122
2.24 : p. 57, 122
2.32 : p. 57
2.36, 41 : p. 57
2.41 : p. 57, 61, 73

2.42 : p. 95
2.46 : p. 58
3.7 : p. 61, 73
3.12ff : p. 61
3.15 : p. 57, 121, 122
3.26 : p. 57
4.2 : p. 122
4.4 : p. 61, 73
4.7–10 : p. 61
4.10 : p. 57
4.31 : p. 122
4.33 : p. 57, 122
5.5, 10 : p. 61
5.20 : p. 122
7.38 : p. 88
7.56 : p. 29, 63
7.58 : p. 34
8.3 : p. 33
8.5ff : p. 62
8.12–17 : p. 123
8.16 : p. 124
8.26ff : p. 95
8.39 : p. 71
9.3 : p. 71
9.3ff : p. 34
9.31 : p. 163
9.34 : p. 73
9.37f : p. 73
10.28 : p. 61
10.41 : p. 56, 71, 122
10.44 : p. 122
10.44f : p. 123
10.44–6 : p. 61
11.3, 17 : p. 61
11.18 : p. 122
12.1ff : p. 61
12.7ff : p. 61, 113
12.17 : p. 62
13.2 : p. 62
13.26ff : p. 122
13.31 : p. 56
13.33 : p. 72, 122
13.34f : p. 122
13.52 : p. 122
14.19ff : p. 113
15.29 : p. 146
16.5ff : p. 62
17.6 : p. 106
17.18, 32 : p. 122
18.9 : p. 71
19.1ff : p. 123
20.7 : p. 57
23.10 : p. 62

23.11 : *p.* 62, 71
23.12 : *p.* 62
25.19 : *p.* 122
26.16 : *p.* 122
27.14ff : *p.* 63
27.23 : *p.* 71
27.23f : *p.* 62
27.24 : *p.* 63
27.24ff : *p.* 113
28.3ff : *p.* 113

ROMANS
1.4 : *p.* 54
1.9 : *p.* 71
6.3 : *p.* 124
6.4 : *p.* 125, 126
6.4f : *p.* 88
6.5 : *p.* 126
8.3 : *p.* 16, 19, 20, 91
8.11 : *p.* 69
8.15 : *p.* 76
8.19–23 : *p.* 177
8.28 : *p.* 178
8.29 : *p.* 91
8.36 : *p.* 87
9.3 : *p.* 87, 146
9.5 : *p.* 47
11.29ff : *p.* 167
12.2 : *p.* 20, 92
12.12 : *p.* 176
15.13 : *p.* 73
15.18f : *p.* 73

I CORINTHIANS
2.4 : *p.* 73
2.9 : *p.* 88
2.16 : *p.* 153
3.21–3 : *p.* 35
4.11–13 : *p.* 100
5.1 : *p.* 67
6.13, 15, 18 : *p.* 67
6.16 : *p.* 32
6.19 : *p.* 126
11.7 : *p.* 91
11.21 : *p.* 67
11.24 : *p.* 38
11.25 : *p.* 52
11.26 : *p.* 38
11.29ff : *p.* 38
12.1–4 : *p.* 68
12.3 : *p.* 44
12.27 : *p.* 164
14.9 : *p.* 67

15.5ff : *p.* 55
15.6 : *p.* 71
15.9 : *p.* 44
15.17 : *p.* 125
15.44f : *p.* 66
16.2 : *p.* 57
16.22 : *p.* 59

II CORINTHIANS
1.5 : *p.* 34
3.17 : *p.* 77
3.17ff : *p.* 69
3.18 : *p.* 77, 91
4.10 : *p.* 88
4.11 : *p.* 89
5.17 : *p.* 69, 151
5.19 : *p.* 167, 177
5.21 : *p.* 21, 87, 91
11.2 : *p.* 32
13.5 : *p.* 126

GALATIANS
1.4 : *p.* 120
1.13 : *p.* 33
2.20 : *p.* 150, 165
3.27 : *p.* 124, 125
4.4–6 : *p.* 76
4.19 : *p.* 150

EPHESIANS
1.10 : *p.* 64, 178
1.20–3 : *p.* 64
1.22 : *p.* 43
1.23 : *p.* 34, 43
2.6 : *p.* 29
2.20 : *p.* 31
2.22 : *p.* 126
3.8 : *p.* 44, 88
3.17, 19 : *p.* 150
4.6 : *p.* 167, 178
4.9, 10 : *p.* 89
4.13 : *p.* 148
4.15, 16 : *p.* 43
5.21 : *p.* 166
5.23 : *p.* 43
5.25ff : *p.* 32
5.28 : *p.* 32
5.29f : *p.* 32
6.18 : *p.* 176

PHILIPPIANS
1.13 : *p.* 63
1.21 : *p.* 35

1.29 : *p.* 87
2.6ff : *p.* 84
2.7 : *p.* 87
2.10–12 : *p.* 64
2.12 : *p.* 163
4.13 : *p.* 35
4.22 : *p.* 63

COLOSSIANS
1.3, 9 : *p.* 177
1.16, 17 : *p.* 64
1.18 : *p.* 43
1.24 : *p.* 34, 87
1.26 : *p.* 168
1.27 : *p.* 150, 168
1.28 : *p.* 177
1.39 : *p.* 176
2.9 : *p.* 34
2.13, 14 : *p.* 120
3.4 : *p.* 150
3.10 : *p.* 91

I THESSALONIANS
2.8 : *p.* 87
5.9f : *p.* 120, 126
5.17 : *p.* 176

I TIMOTHY
1.9 : *p.* 146
1.15 : *p.* 44, 157
4.4 : *p.* 67
4.10 : *p.* 94, 167

II TIMOTHY
1.6 : *p.* 169
1.7 : *p.* 73
1.10 : *p.* 169
2.11f : *p.* 89
3.5 : *p.* 15

TITUS
2.13 : *p.* 63

HEBREWS
1.1–4 : *p.* 153
2.10 : *p.* 102
2.15 : *p.* 120
3.14 : *p.* 126
4.15 : *p.* 21, 91
7.25 : *p.* 168
10.19f : *p.* 120
10.31 : *p.* 155, 163
11.6 : *p.* 172

INDEX OF BIBLICAL REFERENCES

11.17ff : *p.* 100
11.19 : *p.* 144
12.21 : *p.* 163
12.29 : *p.* 155
13.13 : *p.* 100

JAMES
1.8 : *p.* 177
2.16 : *p.* 106

I PETER
2.5 : *p.* 66
3.18 : *p.* 120
4.12f : *p.* 100
4.17 : *p.* 44

II PETER
1.3f : *p.* 74

1.4 : *p.* 126, 149
3. 10–12 : *p.* 46

I JOHN
1.3 : *p.* 71
3.2 : *p.* 149
3.9 : *p.* 126
4.2 : *p.* 68
4.13 : *p.* 126
4.14 : *p.* 167
4.15 : *p.* 68
5.20 : *p.* 126

REVELATION
1.5 : *p.* 120
1.10 : *p.* 57

1.13 : *p.* 29
1.20 : *p.* 63
2.5 : *p.* 63
3.1 : *p.* 45
3.17 : *p.* 45
5.9, 13 : *p.* 59
5.10 : *p.* 89
5.12 : *p.* 59
5.13 : *p.* 59, 63
7.14–17 : *p.* 89
11.15 : *p.* 64
12.10–12 : *p.* 59
19.1f : *p.* 59
19.6 : *p.* 59, 63
21.4 : *p.* 107
22.5 : *p.* 89
22.20 : *p.* 59